BREAKING THROUGH

Using Educational Technology for Children with Special Needs

BARBARA ALBERS HILL

SQUAREONE
PUBLISHERS

Cover Designer: Jeannie Tudor
Cover Photo: Getty Images, Inc.
In-House Editor: Joanne Abrams
Typesetter: Gary A. Rosenberg

Square One Publishers
115 Herricks Road
Garden City Park, NY 11040
(877) 900-BOOK
www.squareonepublishers.com

Library of Congress Cataloging-in-Publication Data

Hill, Barbara Albers.
    Breaking through : using educational technology for children with special
needs / Barbara Albers Hill.
        pages cm
    Includes index.
    ISBN 978-0-7570-0395-0 (pbk.)
    1. Children with disabilities—Education—Computer-assisted instruction.
2. Educational technology. 3. Digital electronics. I. Title.
    LC4024.H55 2014
    371.9—dc23
                                                                2013048294

Printed in the United States of America

10   9   8   7   6   5   4   3   2   1

Contents

Acknowledgments

In the education field, a worthwhile project is never a solo undertaking. A twist on a familiar proverb, "Many hands make *better* work," applies perfectly to the writing of this book. To the many educators, therapists, tech professionals, and friends with whom I collaborated in my teaching career and drew from for this project, thank you for your eagerness to delve into new technology on your students' behalf. The children weren't the only beneficiaries of your initiative and training. I learned so much about tablet technology from watching and working with you, and I appreciate your willingness to share your knowledge and experience.

Teamwork is also embedded in the publishing domain, for good books take shape in an atmosphere of cooperation. To Rudy Shur, Publisher at Square One, thank you for letting me reach out to the many people who live and work with special needs children. Your much-valued confidence in my writing will place a helpful resource in their hands. To Joanne Abrams, Executive Editor and esteemed associate, my thanks for your patience, good humor, and perfectionism. You are a joy to work with, and I'm grateful to have had another chance to draw upon your expertise.

Lastly, special appreciation goes to another faction: my amazing family. To my children, who never mind serving as resources or critiquing ideas and phrasing; and to my husband, who always shares my excitement about my work, thank you. Your encouragement and backing mean more than you know.

A Word About Gender

The child in your life is certainly as likely to be a boy as a girl. However, our language doesn't provide us with a genderless pronoun. To give equal time to both sexes in this book, and to avoid using the awkward "he/she" when referring to your youngster, the feminine pronouns "she," "her," and "hers" have been used in odd-numbered chapters, while the male "he," "him," and "his" appear in all the rest. This decision was made in the interest of simplicity and clarity.

Preface

I spent many years working in the field of special education. During college, I worked with toddlers and preschoolers in a private school. Later, I taught learning disabled teenagers in a public junior high. After that, and for the remainder of my career, I worked as a resource specialist, teaching learning and work strategies to elementary-aged children of varied ability levels. Along the way, I worked to minimize the effects of a host of conditions that hindered my young learners' progress.

As you'd expect, over so many years, I witnessed the advent of many teaching and training techniques and devices, some controversial and some mainstream; some more successful than others at remediating a difficulty or moving past an educational sticking point. However, I can say without hesitation that none has had the immediate and astonishing impact on children that was seen with the introduction of tablet technology.

Children love the tablet's small size, which allows them to handle it easily and carry it from place to place. They respond to the machine's bright colors, sounds, and music, and they're entranced by the touchscreen, which allows them to make things happen with a slide or press of a finger. The game-like aspect of most tablet applications guarantees that fun will be a big part of the user's experience. The machines are fascinating, the apps are multifaceted, and their use involves none of the pressure that is so often a part of learning something new. Children are free to explore, play, and practice to their heart's content in an environment devoid of distraction and the need to be sociable. They're in control, they're being challenged, and they're having a great time. Who can blame them for being enraptured?

This fascination with tablet technology is what makes the machine such a wonderful teaching tool. Simply put, children are eager to use a tablet, and this very fact guarantees the practice that is vital to acquiring a new skill. For special needs children, the impact is even greater. Through an ongoing explosion of apps developed for young users, tablets allow children with social issues, attention deficits, language impairments, and physical problems to move past their challenges so they can interact, communicate, and learn.

It's a very exciting time in the field of special education, and tablet technology is at the forefront. Stories abound about tablet-initiated breakthroughs: the nonverbal child's delight in making his tablet "speak" for him, the youngster with autism enjoying critical practice prior to a social outing, the neurologically challenged child finally grasping the difference between letters and numbers . . . the list goes on and on. In each and every case, a tablet was responsible for the miracle.

Like many parents, teachers, and therapists, I have been surprised and thrilled beyond measure by the unexpected results of this new technology. One simply cannot underestimate the tablet's impact on the social and educational futures of so many children. Yet in my work, I became aware of an information gap that can rob some youngsters of this unmatched opportunity to achieve: Many parents, and even some professionals, may not realize the tremendous growth a tablet can inspire in a special needs child. This book is meant to fill that gap. The information presented in its pages was culled from observations of and interviews with teachers, parents, and assistive technology professionals, as well as through my experiences with students who blossomed under a tablet's influence.

Breaking Through has been created as a tool to help people who live and work with special needs youngsters. The details you are about to read will prepare you to understand, acquire, and employ tablets and apps to help the child in your life become part of this miracle. By combining the right approach with supervised use of carefully chosen programs, you will be able to encourage social relationships, improve critical learning skills, and steer your special needs youngster toward a calmer, happier, more fulfilling life. I wish you the very best in this important endeavor!

Introduction

We all have wants and needs, of course, and we learn early on that their resolution brings comfort and relief. It's a simple matter to ask for what you require or lobby for what you'd like to have. Can you imagine the frustration if most wishes went unmet because you were unable to give voice to them? Imagine further that you found social interaction to be highly irritating. You would weigh every human contact beforehand to assess whether its outcome would be worth your discomfort, and much of the time, you'd probably opt for the safe haven of solitude and silence.

Until recently, these scenarios described everyday life for countless special needs children. The best hope for dealing with their developmental challenges lay in research-based teaching methods and individualized therapies at the hands of skilled professionals. Naturally, families and teachers thrilled at every sign of progress their young charges displayed, but progress was often inconsistent and painfully slow. Then came tablet computers.

The iPad was introduced to the public in 2010 as "the next big thing" in technology. Instantly popular, iPads found their way into classrooms and therapeutic settings as an easy-to-use, highly portable alternative to the mouse-driven PC or Mac and the touch-pad-driven laptop. What wasn't expected was how instantly attractive these tablets would be to children with learning challenges, and how they could work magic to enable communication, socialization, and the acquisition of new skills. Very quickly, parents, teachers, and therapists began looking for ways to give their special needs youngsters access to this riveting new technology.

With the surprising discovery that tablet technology can break down social, physical, and academic barriers, the field of special education has undergone a quiet revolution. Whether a child's learning differences are minimal or extreme, proper use of a tablet and the right applications (apps) can remove roadblocks, facilitate skill development, and improve quality of life—for both children and the adults who care for and teach them.

Today, there are numerous tablets available, along with software that can improve the focus, communication skills, and academic performance of children with developmental and physical challenges. *Breaking Through: Using Educational Technology for Children with Special Needs* has been written to clearly explain the ins and outs of these indispensible devices while helping you pair them with apps that match your child's learning needs. Armed with this information, you'll be able to comfortably put tablet technology to use to engage your child in learning, overcome academic barriers, and maximize his sociability and educational outcome.

Breaking Through is divided into two sections. Part One is composed of four chapters that tell you everything you need to know about using tablet technology. Chapter 1 describes the many features that make tablets so appealing and engaging to a child, from sound and music to action and animation. You'll learn how these elements work together to capture and retain a child's attention, regardless of his learning style, keeping him riveted to and delighted by the activity at hand. The special needs associated with sensory, social, and physical difficulties are also discussed, as tablet technology creates a nonthreatening learning environment that can be modified and controlled to perfectly suit the primary problems accompanying each child's challenges.

Chapter 2 explores the range of learning differences discussed in *Breaking Through*. Challenges such as autism spectrum disorder,

ADHD, hearing impairment, vision impairment, intellectual disability, and traumatic brain injury are identified and described, as are the accompanying needs that lend themselves to technological intervention. The discussion includes the types of apps that can be helpful in each circumstance.

In Chapter 3, I offer suggestions regarding the best ways to introduce, explain, and use tablet technology at home and at school. Included is a helpful list of Do's and Don'ts for parents, caregivers, and teachers.

Chapter 4 provides important information on adapting tablets and their apps to a child's particular needs. You'll be given a look at the types of add-ons and accessories available to extend a tablet's lifespan while specially tailoring it to the sensory preferences and physical capabilities of its user. Part One concludes with a glance at future innovations in the use of tablet technology to help children with learning challenges.

Part Two of *Breaking Through* serves as a complete consumer's guide, providing specifics about tablets, add-ons, and apps. Chapter 5 focuses on tablets. It begins with useful tips to guide your search, and then tells you what to look for in a tablet. Special sections offer money-saving tips, explain the ins and outs of product reviews—where to find them and how to use them—and also fill you in on basic tablet specifications.

Chapter 6 is all about the add-ons and adaptive devices that can enhance the tablet experience of a struggling learner. Specific product recommendations are made for keyboards, styluses, tablet cases, stands and mounts, and other items that can help your child better use and enjoy his tablet.

In Chapter 7, you'll find a complete guide to selecting apps that will not only capture and hold your child's attention but also provide much-needed academic and social development. Included is an extensive list of the best programs available for each learning skill, from organization and scheduling to speech and communication, reading, and much more.

Finally, a helpful Glossary fills you in on terms that may be unfamiliar to you, and a Resources list guides you to the best websites, app stores, and other sources of tablet technology, as well as organizations that offer support and grants for youngsters with developmental and physical challenges.

People who live and work with special needs children know that there are no shortcuts to understanding and resolving learning roadblocks. Therefore, even though *Breaking Through* is divided into handy chapters and sections, each focusing on a specific topic, I urge you to read the entire book rather than skipping to subjects of particular interest. This will give you a fuller understanding of the many possibilities offered by tablet technology and the best way to put this technology to use. Later, when you want to use the book as a reference, its format will help you instantly locate the specific information you need.

Most parents, caregivers, and teachers of special needs children seek to "level the playing field"—that is, to remove or lessen the impact of obstacles such as physical and neurological disabilities so that children can experience greater social and educational development. Today's tablet technology is an ideal path to establishing this equality.

If a child can make greater academic or social strides via technology, he certainly deserves the chance to do so. Sometimes, though, the adults in his life find themselves fixed on a certain plan of action or are simply unaware of available resources for spurring this growth. It is for these individuals and others who live or work with exceptional learners that *Breaking Through* has been written. My hope is that the information, suggestions, and product recommendations contained in its pages will make it an invaluable resource for everyone who seeks to lessen life's many challenges for special children.

PART ONE

Understanding the Basics

Parents and professionals have made the surprising discovery that tablet computers and applications can help overcome the primary learning problems that accompany many social, neurological, and physical disabilities. Part One of *Breaking Through* provides fundamental information about the use of tablet technology by special needs kids and presents helpful suggestions for getting children started on their own tablet adventures.

The four chapters that follow will help you understand why and how a tablet can maximize your child's progress in communication and learning. You will also discover the best ways to introduce and oversee your child's use of this technology, and—just as important—you'll learn what *not* to do when supervising or working with your child. Finally, you'll get a look at the ways in which you can make your youngster's tablet more accessible to his needs and able to withstand daily use by his curious hands. Read on to learn how you can best help your child enjoy the many advantages a tablet has to offer.

1

The Unique World of Tablet Technology

Sasha was born with *cortical visual impairment (CVI)*, a neurological condition that prevents her from properly processing things that appear in her line of sight. She often looks as if she is blind, because she never looks at people's faces and doesn't respond to objects unless she is able to touch them. For Sasha, seeing isn't instinctive as it is for most people; in fact, it requires tremendous effort. She finds it easiest to perceive bright lights and high contrast, and she is able to register moving items better than stationary ones, particularly if they are reflective. Sasha has full perception of color but is quickly fatigued by trying to make sense of visual information. She has the greatest success when viewing a single image on an illuminated white background. Needless to say, Sasha's CVI makes learning an incredible challenge for her.

This year, Sasha's school introduced iPads in their special education classrooms. Sasha was immediately fascinated by the brightly lit screen, and she quickly learned that she could control the color, movement, and sound by tapping and sliding her finger. Eight months later, she remains captivated by the device, and her teachers and parents report that she is learning to interpret images as never before.

The ease of use afforded by a tablet's high contrast has jumpstarted Sasha's pace of learning. For other special needs children, it may be a different feature or combination of elements that holds the key to breaking through a social or educational barrier. Chapter 1 explores the incredible appeal that tablets hold for all types of learners. You'll learn that today's children feel at ease with technology in general and have a special fascination with a tablet's interactive capabilities. You'll also discover why such a wonderful match exists between special needs children and tablet technology when software is chosen and introduced in a manner that is just right for each learner. Finally, you'll get a fast look at the skill development that can be achieved through use of a tablet and apps.

WHY DO CHILDREN FIND TECHNOLOGY SO APPEALING?

It is hardly a secret that today's children are drawn to computers. Born in the digital age and surrounded by technology virtually from birth, they feel none of the intimidation adults often experience when learning to use a new device. Children view technology as being there for their exploration, and, unlike older users, they don't hesitate to experiment. They press buttons, change screens, click the mouse, and otherwise take what adult novices view as risks. Why? Because digital-age children instinctively understand that if they make a mistake, they won't do any permanent damage. Almost any wrong move can be undone so that a new, more successful move can be attempted.

Free of the fear that holds back older computer users, children simply revel in what technology has to offer. The use of color, sound, and animation makes children's software stimulating, attention-grabbing, and instantly attractive, no matter what a child's learning style. Visual learners love the lights, color, and moving images; auditory learners respond to the music, conversation, and trigger sounds; and tactile learners enjoy controlling the mouse or joystick. Simply put, children's software contains something for every learning style, and using it is fun!

The interactive aspect of computer software increases its appeal to children. Games and programs often pause for a youngster's response, and the fact that she has a specific role to play increases her interest and holds her attention. If the child presses a key or clicks the mouse, something happens that *she* initiated. Objects move and noises occur, and she must make sense of what is on the screen and use what she knows of the world to plan her next move. A child's deep concentration while at the computer is all the evidence we need that the activity is both motivating and rewarding.

Computer technology seems to hold an even greater appeal for many children with special needs. Whether a child's challenge relates to language, socialization, or a physical or neurological issue, the computer offers a new approach to interaction. Distractions are forgotten, troubling social pressures fade away, and active participation is encouraged in a way that eliminates the fear of failure and promotes discovery. The engaging elements of children's software capture and hold almost every child's attention, and programs offer visual and verbal reinforcement that is both pleasing and important to learning. When a child uses a computer, she moves into an entertaining and enjoyable world. For the special needs child, this is often a place that soothes, relaxes, and affords social interaction, play, or movement that may be missing from her everyday life.

THE SPECIAL APPEAL OF THE TABLET COMPUTER

For children, the tablet is an even more dynamic device than a desktop or laptop computer. There is no delay between watching your efforts on the keyboard, joystick, mouse, or touchpad and looking up to see the onscreen result. Instead, there are instantaneous results from hand movements that are simple and intuitive. A child merely needs to point (tap) at what is wanted, push (swipe) away what isn't, and explore items on the screen just as she would if they were three-dimensional objects. All of these motions mirror everyday gestures, and youngsters quickly adapt to and enjoy the cause-and-effect aspect of their hand or stylus movements on the screen. In short, the tablet enables a direct and pleasing connection that is missing when you use a standard mouse, touchpad, or other cursor-enabling device. Additionally, the effort and skill needed to manipulate these tools has been eliminated.

There is a virtually unlimited supply of tablet applications for children, with more becoming available every day. Many such apps have been developed by parents and child-development professionals—people who truly understand what attracts and motivates a youngster. Some of these apps are free, and many of the rest are inexpensive when compared with programs for a PC, Mac, or laptop. As you would expect, this wealth of software translates into a wonderful variety of activities that are literally at a child's fingertips. This, in turn, increases the likelihood of further exploration and learning.

Perhaps most important, the tablet is small and lightweight and, therefore, easier to carry around than a laptop. The fact that a tablet can accompany a child on a car ride, visit, or outing is an attractive feature that usually translates into additional use. As friends, relatives, and passers-by remark on the device or the skill with which it is being used, many children enjoy a boost in self-esteem and a special feeling of possessiveness about their machine. This encourages even more use and keeps the cycle of fascination going. For all of these reasons, tablet technology just "clicks" with children.

TABLETS AND LEARNING CHALLENGES

Much speculation has gone into why tablets are particularly engaging—and so very helpful—to children with special needs. The factors mentioned above come into play, of course, but a tablet also provides sensory stimulation that so many struggling youngsters crave. The very nature of most children's apps means that there is a constant stream of sights, sounds, and movement. When an activity is carefully selected and introduced in manageable segments, the child's attention is captured and held in a way that enables her to learn both the use of the machine and the targeted skill. The child gets immediate, rewarding feedback and soon learns how to control the activity at hand. With adult guidance, the usual resistance to learning something new simply disappears when a tablet is the mode of practice.

Tablet apps can be tailored to a child's individual needs. For instance, by limiting the number of onscreen choices or setting a level of difficulty, the app can be geared to instruct her rather than frustrate her. Because the apps are so inexpensive and abundant, parents and teachers can find countless ways to practice every imaginable skill at any performance level.

Tablets are lightweight and easy to hold, and protective coverings can be added to guard against damage during use by a child. The interactive screen replaces a mouse and keyboard, and this can appeal to children with visual or motor challenges. (As you'll see in Chapter 4, assistive add-ons are available for youngsters who lack the dexterity to succeed with a touchscreen.) Ultimately, the ease of use offered by the tablet creates a more positive learning environment. Tablets and the right applications can also replace the more expensive and cumbersome light boxes, traditional speech generating devices, and adapted PCs that have been the mainstays of special education for many years.

Tablets work wonders for the parents and teachers of special needs children, too. Many apps have built-in progress monitoring, which means that you don't have to spend time assessing improvement and keeping records. A tablet can be used by several children through the addition of tabs that guide each user to her own specially selected programs. Finally, young users are often calmer, more attentive, and more eager to pursue a tablet activity than they would be if they practiced the skill in a more tradional manner, making teaching and learning much easier. And when a child enjoys a faster rate of progress, everyone's goals are met.

POSSIBILITIES AND OUTCOMES

Children with learning challenges have so very much to gain from monitored access to a tablet computer, careful teaching of its use, and a thoughtful selection of apps geared to their developmental needs. Reports abound of the enormous educational progress made by children who have a broad range of conditions and diagnoses.

Communication can be enabled and enhanced when the tablet is used as an *augmentative and alternative communication (AAC)* device. A child can respond to questions by touching the associated onscreen icon, or she can piece together a sentence by tapping a succession of images. The camera feature of a tablet allows the child to use pictures or video to tell a story or relate a chain of events. In so many cases, children who struggle to speak are now able to communicate through this new technology.

With a tablet, children with learning difficulties can receive vision training; enhance their vocabulary and spelling; develop their grasp of grammar, reading, and writing; or practice math and money skills. In addition, they can learn daily living skills, including hygiene and self-care; develop social skills, such as *pragmatics* (the use of appropriate language in different social situations); and even receive vocational preparation. A child can work at her current achievement level without fear of social stigma; in fact, her use of a tablet may increase her status in the eyes of classmates and peers. Although using educational apps isn't always easy and automatic, with time and teaching, the young tablet user enjoys a satisfying ability to control her learning environment. She is also able to employ creativity as she explores and becomes adept at the chosen programs.

Special needs tablet users show greater growth in communication, socialization, and academic skills. As a result, they also experience a boost in self-esteem. The increasing numbers of parents and teachers who delight in their child's happiness, improved focus, and academic or social progress are another consequence that is nearly as important!

CONCLUSION

Today's children simply "get" technology. Their experiences make them very much at ease with computers, and for most, learning the routines and skills needed to use a tablet is a natural and pleasurable process. A perfect illustration of this comfort level with technology can be seen in the October 2011 YouTube video "A Magazine Is an iPad That Does Not Work." The much-viewed video shows a baby repeatedly trying to press and swipe the unresponsive pictures in a magazine. When nothing happens, she turns away and pushes the periodical aside. Another video, "Baby Swiping at TV," from February 2013, shows a toddler using his finger to try to scroll down through video listings appearing on his TV screen. When he can't make things happen onscreen, he moves his hand to the buttons on the side of the machine to try his luck there. In both instances, the babies are visibly surprised that the expected fingertip control is absent.

The examples of infant behavior described above highlight a concern that some people have regarding the use of tablets by young children. Some experts worry that this technology may have negative effects on developing minds, a topic that is explored further in Chapter 3. Certainly, computers should not replace real-life activities. Children need time playing with physical objects so they can learn how the world works, just as they need to interact with other people. But, depending on their disability, special needs children may have difficulty exploring or understanding the world and communicating with others. In their case, the interactive aspect of tablets can help them break through obstacles posed by physical or developmental challenges, allowing them to better connect with the world and people around them. Tablets and apps are certainly fun to use, although a period of learning is often involved before a child can navigate a program independently. The key to success is the selection of targeted apps that teach as well as fascinate, and adults who knowledgeably supervise a child's work time.

For youngsters with special needs, tablets and their applications possess an undeniable power that can spur learning and yield other life-enhancing benefits. Chapter 2 explores the various learning challenges that can affect a child's skill development and briefly explains the ways in which tablet technology can reach and help these children.

2

Special Needs and Tablet Technology

Thomas was diagnosed with autistic disorder at the age of twenty months. At three-and-a-half, he remained nonverbal and spent much of each day frustrated and crying in anger. The more his parents tried to guess the causes of his unhappiness, the more inconsolable he became. Soon, his tantrums were lasting up to an hour or more.

Then, at a family gathering, Thomas spotted his aunt's iPad. Enthralled by his ability to create sounds and move pictures on the device, Thomas spent his first peaceful afternoon in months experimenting with the machine's touchscreen. His parents, amazed by his sudden calm and delighted by his fascination with the device, decided to invest in a tablet for his use. With training, Thomas was soon using an application that helped him express himself as he never could before. Today, he carries the tablet everywhere and uses it for communication. His newfound ability to convey his thoughts and feelings has alleviated much of his former frustration, and tantrums are now a rarity. Thomas's parents are thrilled by their child's increased independence, and the whole family is enjoying the much-improved atmosphere at home.

Thomas is but one of many children who can enjoy improved communication, better focus, enhanced social interactions, and faster skill development through the use of a tablet computer. Of course, there are many challenges other than autism that can lead to a child's having special learning needs. Some of these are physical conditions, others are neurologically or emotionally based issues, and still others are related to speech quality. While some of these difficulties may be present at birth, others can be acquired afterward or simply diagnosed long after the fact.

This chapter offers a look at ten conditions that can have a significant impact on a child's interactions, development, and learning. Background information is provided for each diagnosis, along with an overview of the roadblocks to development that are so often associated with the problem. In addition, you'll get a look at the accompanying learning needs that lend themselves to supervised use of tablets and apps.

AUTISM SPECTRUM DISORDER

Autism spectrum disorders (ASDs) are neurologically based conditions that impair communication, socialization, and behavior. Because ASDs are developmental delays, they are initially hard to pinpoint, and diagnosis can be difficult. In addition, a child's symptoms can change with maturity and teaching. The learning needs that accompany an ASD tend to be numerous and varied; therefore, approaches to intervention often differ greatly from one child to the next. ASDs are classified according to the number and degree of symptoms. They include Pervasive Developmental Disorder Not Otherwise Specified (PDD-NOS), Asperger syndrome, and autistic disorder, all of which are described below.

Pervasive Developmental Disorder Not Otherwise Specified (PDD-NOS). Sometimes called atypical autism, PDD-NOS causes a child to exhibit some signs of autism but not in sufficient intensity or number to warrant the label of Asperger syndrome or autistic disorder. Nevertheless, problem behaviors such as poor eye contact, lack of attention, unusual vocal tone or pitch, and anxiety still affect the child's social abilities and academic growth.

Asperger Syndrome. The chief characteristic of *Asperger syndrome* is difficulty in handling social situations. Although children with Asperger often have above-average intelligence and experience no delay in learning speech—in fact, they often use vocabulary that is advanced for their age—they tend to speak in a monotone. Because they interpret language literally, they also may have trouble understanding and using colloquial language and figures of speech. Eye contact is generally poor, and the child's interaction with other people is direct and intense, lacking the easy give-and-take of most social relationships. In conversation, the child tends to fixate on and repeat one or two ideas without regard to the listener's interest or response.

Autistic Disorder. Children with *autistic disorder*—the most severe form of ASD—experience problems with focus, communication, and socialization. Commonly, they use unusual or repetitive behaviors to either stimulate or calm themselves. Because repetition is so important to them, they are often unable to accept any change in routine. Despite intellectual ability that is usually in the average range, the great majority of children with autistic disorder have academic problems due to a lack of attention and a tendency toward concrete, literal thinking. Many autistic children are without abstract reasoning skills. Egocentric, they think only of themselves, lack empathy, and are unaware of the impact that their behavior has on others.

As with Thomas, whose story opened this chapter, tablet technology has been surprisingly successful at enhancing focus, communication, social awareness, and academic skills in children with all forms of ASD. Tablet use eliminates the need for the verbal interactions that can be so difficult, and the constant flow of visual and auditory stimulation works well to capture and hold the child's attention. An abundance of applications are available to target the language delays, social skills, attentional difficulties, and other learning roadblocks that are common among children on the autism spectrum. In addition, many autistic children appear to exhibit a reduction in anxiety when they work on a tablet.

LEARNING DISABILITY

Learning disabilities (LDs), which are sometimes referred to as learning differences, encompass a large variety of academic and pre-academic skills. LD children usually have average or above-average intellectual ability; however, they process visual and/or auditory information differently from most children. A learning disability can exist in the area of reading, writing, math, speaking, or listening, or it can surface as a disorder of *executive function* (the higher-order skills needed to plan, organize, and think abstractly). This wide range of potential problems means that recognizing an LD can be tricky. Generally speaking, the hallmark of an LD is an obvious deficit in one or more skill areas as compared with a child's overall ability level.

Approaches to remediating LDs have long centered on multi-sensory instruction and the teaching of *compensatory strategies*—strategies designed to bypass the problem. However, recent research shows that the brain's *neuroplasticity,* or lifelong ability to change and restore itself, allows it under ideal conditions to form new nerve connections that enable the learning of previously difficult tasks. This means that there may be the potential to actually *lessen* a disability rather than sidestepping it. With this knowledge and the use of tablet technology have come many new possibilities for LD children.

Using a tablet and the right applications, a child with a learning disability can get repeated practice with vocabulary development, the recognition of letters and sound, direction following, and the memorization of math facts. The nature of the tablet encourages improved focus and better concentration, both of which are extremely important to a struggling learner. Fine motor control can be improved, as can the child's ability to identify and process sounds and visual information. In addition, tablets and apps can be used for scheduling, organizing, and practicing a host of specific academic skills.

INTELLECTUAL DISABILITY

Once referred to as mental retardation, *intellectual disability (ID)* involves below-average cognition, a slowed paced of learning, and adaptive behaviors (everyday skills of living) that lag behind those of people of the same age. A child's level of ID is linked to his ability to reason, plan, and solve problems—all of which are measured by his IQ (intelligence quotient)—and can range from mild to profound.

Signs of an ID first become apparent in a youngster's inability to achieve developmental milestones, such as crawling and babbling in a timely way; behavior problems; and difficulty with logic and memory. In the most severe instances, there may be additional physical problems involving vision, hearing, or motor skills.

An intellectual disability can be genetically based, as with Down syndrome, or it can be linked to problems with fetal development due to illness, poor nutrition, substance abuse, or environmental factors. Very premature birth or oxygen deprivation during delivery can also cause ID. In addition, severe infection, brain injury, or a home environment lacking in stimulation and nurturing can bring about this problem in children who were born with average intellectual capabilities.

Tablet technology has undeniable benefits for children with ID. Numerous apps provide fine motor practice, assistance with speaking and understanding language, the teaching of routines, familiarization with people and objects, and the learning of social and self-care skills. There are also apps designed to enhance focus and memorization, which can lead to improved academic skills. For a nonverbal child, the tablet can aid communication and improve social interaction, which ultimately can enhance self-esteem.

ANXIETY DISORDER

Anxiety disorder goes well beyond the classic nervous feelings that most young children experience when confronted with unfamiliar faces, new situations, or such environmental triggers as animals or thunder and lightning. When worry becomes constant, overpowering, and disabling and affects a child's everyday life, anxiety disorder may be the culprit. Anxiety disorder that occurs in children falls into six categories, as follows.

Generalized Anxiety Disorder. A child with *generalized anxiety disorder* exhibits extreme free-floating worry and agitation over a period of six months or longer, even if there is little or nothing to cause the anxiety.

Separation Anxiety Disorder. A youngster with *separation anxiety disorder* experiences significant, prolonged distress when separated from a parent or primary caregiver.

Social Anxiety Disorder. A child with *social anxiety disorder* has an unreasonable and excessive fear of social situations in which he might be watched and judged by other people.

Obsessive-Compulsive Disorder. A child with *obsessive-compulsive disorder (OCD)* is plagued by fears, and eases his anxiety by performing certain rituals or routines. He may count, check and recheck things, or repeat words or actions in order to manage his own thoughts.

Phobia. A phobic child experiences an unreasonable, overwhelming fear of a specific situation or thing. Dogs, ocean waves, clowns, and insects—among many other things—have been known to provoke phobic reactions.

Post-Traumatic Stress Disorder. A child with *post-traumatic stress disorder (PTSD)* exhibits extreme fear and anxiety for months after a frightening incident. Common signs of this disorder include the complete avoidance of people and a refusal to separate from parents.

Children with anxiety disorders can find relief from symptoms and improve their condition by working with tablet technology.

There are many apps that enable a child to practice and prepare for particular situations, including social conversation. The tablet also allows a child with anxiety disorder to gradually develop or restore social contact with peers by first sharing apps and games for which no conversation is needed. In addition, a tablet can provide repeated exposure to books, stories, and games about fear and shyness. As the child sees his own progress and achievement, he experiences a helpful boost in self-esteem.

ATTENTION DEFICIT HYPERACTIVITY DISORDER

Attention Deficit Hyperactivity Disorder (ADHD) can be a byproduct of many of the diagnoses and conditions discussed earlier in the chapter. However, its impact on a child's learning is so pervasive that, for the purposes of this chapter, it is being considered as a separate disorder.

ADHD can exist with or without the hyperactivity component. Often, the disorder isn't diagnosed until the start of formal schooling, because periodic impulsive, excitable, and overly energetic behavior is characteristic of most toddlers and preschoolers. Usually, maturity resolves overactivity, so doctors often wait out this developmental phase before considering an ADHD diagnosis.

ADHD can involve a range of behaviors that can vary in severity from mild to severe. An ADHD child may be in constant motion, running, jumping, jiggling, and squirming, unable to remain still even long enough to eat a meal. Trouble sleeping is another common characteristic. ADHD children who lack the hyperactivity component are nowhere near as active; however, they have trouble maintaining eye contact and are unable to stay focused on activities because their attention is summoned by every sound or movement around them.

Children with ADHD are easily overstimulated and very difficult to calm. The presence of too much visual, auditory, or tactile information often leads to tantrums or aggression that can't be controlled until the child exhausts himself. Also, impulsiveness is magnified in an ADHD child, making him seem unaware of risks, prone to accidents, and in need of constant supervision.

Tablet technology has been shown to have an immediate and surprising effect on children with ADHD. The device's constant stream of sights and sounds seems to override the youngster's inability to pay attention and maintain eye contact. ADHD children who thrive on constant motion are entranced by the high energy portrayed in many apps and find the interactive feature both pleasing and engaging. By harnessing the attention of an ADHD child, a tablet offers limitless learning possibilities.

SPEECH/LANGUAGE IMPAIRMENT

Speech difficulties are separate from language disorders yet are grouped under the same umbrella of *speech/language impairment (SLI)*. Speech difficulties involve errors in sound or word production, fluency, or vocal quality. Language issues, on the other hand, are characterized by difficulty in recognizing and understanding words or using words in sentences. No clear causes have been found for SLI that occurs apart from biological conditions such as hearing loss, but there appears to be a hereditary component. It has been estimated that 75 percent of children with an SLI have a family member who also has an SLI.

Understandably, there are social consequences to having impaired speech. SLI children can be difficult or impossible to understand, which limits their interactions with other children. Every day, they experience frustration as they try and fail to make themselves understood. Language issues have an impact on reading, writing, and learning. More than 40 percent of children with language impairment have trouble learning to read due to an incomplete grasp of vocabulary and verb tenses, or have difficulty processing language and other auditory information.

The obstacles to learning that are involved in SLI mesh nicely with tablet technology. The device's inherent instant feedback encourages a child to keep trying a difficult task that he might otherwise abandon because there seemed to be no reward. Practicing speech or language skills on a tablet is risk-free, unlike attempts to talk to peers, who are less supportive. In addition, a tablet provides many more opportunities to practice speaking and listening than an SLI child could get through social interaction. Many apps are available for broadening vocabulary, improving the pronunciation of words, practicing fluent speech, and listening to and following verbal directions. In addition, there are apps for reinforcing grammar and verb tenses, and still others that provide the older child with help in organizing his thoughts and applying proper *mechanics*—spelling, punctuation, and the like—to his written work.

VISUAL IMPAIRMENT

The term *visual impairment (VI)* is used to describe any type of vision loss, whether total or partial. There are two categories of VI—cortical visual impairment and low vision.

Cortical Visual Impairment. Sometimes, VI is the result of *cortical visual impairment (CVI)*, a disorder linked to a problem in the brain rather than the eye. CVI makes it extremely difficult for a child to focus on and interpret visual information. Sometimes called cortical blindness, this disorder presents as partial vision that fluctuates greatly throughout the day and usually involves limitations in the visual field. CVI can be caused by problems with oxygenation or blood supply during birth, infections such as encephalitis or meningitis, a stroke or other injury to the brain, or a brain abnormality.

Low Vision. Visual impairment can also be a function of *low vision*, which is partial vision loss that can't be corrected with regular eyeglasses or contact lenses. A child's low vision can manifest as a peripheral (side) vision limitation or a problem with visual acuity—that is, the clarity with which the child sees objects in his environment. Causes of low vision in children include abnormalities of the retina or optic nerve; pediatric glaucoma or cataracts; albinism; and nystagmus, or uncontrolled eye movement. An examination by a pediatric ophthalmologist can determine whether the low vision is degenerative and if some type of corrective lenses would help.

Tablet technology is proving very beneficial to children with both types of visual impairment. The tablet allows them to magnify pictures and words, adjust the brightness of the screen, and change colors and tints to enhance visibility. The high contrast makes focusing easier, which translates into increased usage of the device and, ultimately, a greater ability to recognize and understand what appears on the screen. Exciting research suggests that the proper use of tablets and apps by visually impaired children encourages brain cell growth, which, in turn, can lead to permanent improvement in a child's ability to recognize and interpret visual information.

HEARING IMPAIRMENT

A loss in hearing that prevents an individual from normally receiving or processing sounds is referred to as *hearing impairment (HI)*. This condition can be present at birth or occur later in life and can result from pregnancy or birth issues, infection, medication, injury to the brain or ear, a genetic disorder, or exposure to extreme noise. The degree of hearing loss can vary widely, from partial to complete, depending on a child's individual circumstances. Although it is often associated with damage to the ear, it can be caused by damage to other structures, as well. HI is generally divided into four categories.

Central Hearing Impairment. In *central HI,* the ear itself works correctly, but damage has occurred in the central nervous system, either in the brain itself or in pathways to the brain. This impairs the child's ability to recognize and interpret sounds and language.

In a related condition called *auditory processing disorder (APD)*, a child's hearing is normal, but he has difficulty isolating, understanding, and responding to sounds and language from his environment and thus has difficulty learning.

Conductive Hearing Impairment. *Conductive HI* is caused by a physical problem in the outer or middle ear—the pathways through which sound reaches the inner ear. Because sound can't easily be transmitted through the ear, it is lower and more difficult to perceive.

Sensorineural Hearing Impairment. *Sensorineural HI* refers to a problem with the *cochlea*—the organ of balance and hearing found in the inner ear—and/or the auditory nerve that supplies it. Sounds and speech can be either muffled and hard to understand, or distorted and "scrambled."

Mixed Hearing Impairment. *Mixed HI* is a combination of sensorineural and conductive hearing loss. This means that there is damage to both the inner ear and the outer or middle ear, causing sound information to the brain to be both suppressed and disorganized.

Whatever the reason for a child's struggle to hear and process auditory information, tablet technology is proving invaluable at providing assistance. When using a tablet, children with HI show an improved ability to focus, and specific applications offer many opportunities for identifying sounds, understanding spoken language, practicing speech, and developing vocabulary. In severe cases of HI, captioning and voice recognition software can also provide help. And with a child's improved ability to communicate comes greater social success and stronger self-esteem.

TRAUMATIC BRAIN INJURY

Traumatic brain injury (TBI), referred to in its milder form as *concussion*, is an injury to the brain caused by an external blow to the skull or a violent forward-and-backward whipping of the head. TBI causes stretching and shearing of the nerves in the brain, which, in turn, disrupts normal brain function. By definition, a TBI excludes degenerative conditions, congenital problems, and birth-related

25

injuries. The degree and nature of its effects depend on the force of the blow and the area affected.

Signs of TBI are wide ranging and vary greatly in severity. It is often said that no two such injuries are the same, nor are the post-concussive effects, which, in some cases, linger for years or become permanent. TBI can lead to physical disabilities, sensory problems, problems with thinking, social or emotional issues, and behavioral changes. Because the brain's *neuroplasticity*, or ability to restore itself, may enable the brain injury to heal, it is hard to predict the extent or duration of a child's recovery from a TBI. It is important to remember that residual post-concussive problems may not surface until later in a child's development, when higher-level cognitive skills come into play.

Tablet technology has been shown to be extremely helpful to children with TBI. Many apps can help improve short-term memory and reteach vocabulary. Apps can also be used to practice and thereby familiarize the TBI child with everyday tasks or situations. There is software that reinforces scheduling, tracking, and list-making, which may be necessary to help with personal organization. Many apps offer fine motor practice, reinforce pre-academic and academic skills, or chart a child's behavior. In addition, an abundance of software has been designed to enhance a TBI child's speech and language skills and attention span.

ORTHOPEDIC IMPAIRMENT

An *orthopedic impairment (OI)* is a problem within a child's musculoskeletal system—the system of bones, joints, muscles, tendons, and ligaments that enable the body to move. Included under this umbrella term are congenital conditions such as a missing limb or osteogenesis imperfecta (brittle bone disease); problems stemming from an illness such as poliomyelitis (polio); and difficulties that are due to other causes, such as fractures, amputation, or cerebral palsy. Some OIs exist before birth, but other conditions are acquired through accident, injury, or premature birth. There are many dif-

26

ferent OIs, which vary greatly in severity. Generally, OIs are subdivided into the following three classifications.

Degenerative Diseases. This category covers conditions such as muscular dystrophy, multiple sclerosis, and osteoarthritis—diseases that are characterized by the deterioration of organs or tissues over time. Degenerative diseases have a progressive and increasing impact on a child's motor skills.

Neuromotor Impairments. Disorders in this category are characterized by problems with the spinal cord, brain, or nervous system that are acquired at or prior to birth and affect a child's ability to control, feel, or use certain parts of his body. Spina bifida and cerebral palsy are examples of neuromotor impairment.

Musculoskeletal Disorders. This category covers diseases and conditions that involve the muscles and bones, such as a clubfoot or a missing limb. Musculoskeletal disorders may be present at birth or can result from an accident or injury. Surgery, prosthetics, orthotics, or the use of a wheelchair may be factors in the life of a child with a musculoskeletal condition.

The motor limitations that accompany orthopedic impairment vary widely from motor skill weakness to poorly controlled movement to total immobility. Multiple disabilities are not uncommon in cases of OI, and some children exhibit accompanying speech problems. Naturally, the level of learning needs is equally varied, sometimes calling for creative and extensive intervention. In some cases, there is the added challenge of facing chronic or terminal illness.

Children with OI can benefit greatly from tablets and apps. They can practice important fine motor skills, work on developing speech and language, and get valuable practice with pre-academic and academic skills. Apps are available to help older children better express themselves verbally or in writing. There is also a great deal of software that can provide exposure to the world, which OI children may miss due to poor mobility and an inability to participate in traditional childhood play. In addition, apps are a good way to share self-esteem-boosting stories about other OI children and their accomplishments.

CONCLUSION

The information presented in this chapter provides a snapshot of the various roadblocks to socialization and learning that face special needs youngsters. Once you understand these developmental barriers, it is easy to see the value of any tactic or device that can hasten growth and minimize the emotional toll that almost always accompanies learning challenges. It is for this reason that tablet computers have proven to be such an exciting development in the field of special education.

If a tablet seems like it may benefit the very special child in your life, it is certainly advisable to introduce and use it in the best way possible. Chapter 3 will guide you in teaching and overseeing the use of this very special technology.

3

Maximizing
Tablet Use

Kayla was four years old when the car she was riding in was struck from behind at a stoplight. Despite the fact that Kayla was restrained in a car seat, the force of the collision caused her head to whip forward, snap back against the rear of the seat, and then fly forward again. Kayla was unconscious for several minutes and was transported to a nearby emergency room for evaluation. The diagnosis was a mild traumatic brain injury (TBI), also called concussion, caused by Kayla's brain slamming against the inside rear of her skull, then the front, then the rear again during her head's violent movement after the collision.

One year later, Kayla is still recovering from her TBI. Her biggest post-concussive problem has been remembering the names of people and objects, a difficulty which is magnified in public settings that involve multiple conversations. Fearing the social consequences of their daughter's word-finding problem, Kayla's parents sought advice from her therapists about ways they could help at home. Eventually, they bought a tablet computer with image-naming capabilities and an application that creates pictures, flashcards, and storyboards. However, this purchase triggered a new concern: Could the family manage Kayla's tablet use so that onscreen work remained just one of numerous activities in the child's day? The answer to their question was "Yes." Kayla now spends thirty minutes a day on the tablet using photos of familiar objects and people for naming practice. She checks her responses and makes corrections with the machine's voice-over feature. Kayla enjoys the activity's challenge and loves keeping track of her correct responses. She also has no problem walking away from the device when work time is over, because her parents established ground rules about the tablet's use right from the start.

Lately, Kayla's speech is beginning to sound more fluent. She also appears to be more relaxed at social gatherings and has started initiating conversations just as she did before the car accident. Her parents are thrilled by the improvement in their daughter's conversational skills, and they point to her work on the tablet—and their own careful oversight of her daily practice—as the reason for her success.

Work with tablets and apps can spearhead similar improvement in the communication or learning skills of numerous special needs children, regardless of the reason for their struggles. Evidence shows that success is greatest when the device is viewed as an educational tool rather than an entertainment source. This chapter presents valuable suggestions for preparing for, introducing, and monitoring your youngster's practice with the helpful and therapeutic apps she needs. It also offers a look at the potential problems that can accompany tablet use by children, along with information on how to avoid these pitfalls. Finally, you'll find a concise list of "Do's" and "Don'ts" especially geared to guide a young tablet user. If you are ready to make tablet technology a part of your special child's skill development, read on to learn the best way to proceed.

GETTING READY

The purchase of a tablet computer involves a considerable sum of money. Naturally, parents and teachers hope for the best possible return on this investment. Whether the child who will be using the device is two years old or twelve, a smooth and stress-free introduction to the new machine will be key to ensuring her excitement and interest. This is best accomplished when the supervising adult is completely familiar with the tablet and has a well-thought-out plan for its use.

Before buying a tablet, it is wise to learn about the many features of these computers and consider exactly how yours will be used. How roughly do you expect your child to handle the machine? Models vary widely in levels of impact-resistance, and you may choose to include a sturdy case and screen protector in your purchase. (Additional information about improving a machine's durability is provided in Chapter 4.) How important or necessary are features such as a built-in camera or enhanced visual display, both of which will add to the cost? Are 32GB of memory sufficient, or do you need 64GB? Depending on where you live, you may wish to buy a device with 4G connectivity for faster, more reliable internet access. Or you may feel that 3G is perfectly fine. Finally, does your child have motor problems that would make assistive devices necessary for her to successfully use a tablet? (Please see Chapter 4 for more about helpful add-ons.) The answers to these questions will vary according to individual taste, your budget, your child's needs, and the location in which your tablet will be used. You should discuss the specifics of your pending purchase, not just with a salesperson but also with a technology professional whose answers you trust. The initial cost of tablet ownership is significant and may warrant a second or third opinion. (For more help in choosing a tablet, see Chapter 5.)

Once you buy a tablet, it is recommended that you explore—or get a lesson in—all the features of the device that can maximize its appeal to your child. Checking under "Settings," finding an online tutorial for your model name and number, or reviewing the printed material that was enclosed with the device can be very helpful in this regard. Look for ways to adjust the brightness of the screen, font size, voice selection, speech rate, and text and background colors. Also, you may be able to set up assistive touch, choose a plain background, or lock your screen to keep it from reorienting when it's moved around, all of which can make the tablet easier for your child to manage.

Finally, it is important to set up your tablet before showing it to your child. This gives you the chance to establish desired restrictions, organize the quantity of folders that seems best for your young learner, and download the applications you have chosen to use at the start. If passwords are an option on your device, it is recommended that you set one for unlocking the screen and share it with your child as appropriate. Then create a separate, secret code that covers settings and restrictions. This initial work will help you become completely familiar with your machine before presenting it to your child. It will also keep control of the tablet's features and apps within your adult hands.

INTRODUCING THE TABLET

While the sight of any new item will initially intrigue most children, and while tablet computers are known for their attention-getting features, the many steps required for their safe and appropriate use can easily be overwhelming. Unless your child is very young or has developmental delays that make it difficult to learn or follow routines, it is a good idea to introduce the tablet gradually. Rather than summoning your child for her first look at an app in progress, or even a powered-on screen, it is better to provide step-by-step exposure to the machine and all it can do. Your child will have a better understanding of the tablet and its educational powers and become a more proficient user if she learns about the device before she becomes captivated by its apps.

Your child's age, developmental readiness, and attention level can guide you in deciding which step-by-step elements are appropriate to teach, as well as how long each work session should be. In many cases, five minutes may initially be enough, particularly if your child tends to resist one-to-one interaction or has difficulty maintaining focus and loses interest easily. Again, the magnitude of your investment in a tablet makes it important to move slowly, and there is much to be said for powering down and putting away your device before your child becomes annoyed by the details or by your efforts to engage her attention. Here are some steps you may wish to follow as you introduce your new tablet to your youngster. Please note that if this approach is not appropriate at this time, you can always introduce tablet usage and care elements later, when your child is ready to participate.

With your child seated beside you, take out the tablet and describe it as a special machine that can help the family learn and do new things. Point out that it is small and lightweight, which means that family members have to be very careful when they touch it. Open the cover (if applicable), explain how it protects the machine, and point out the screen, the charger, and the button that turns the power on. If appropriate, invite your child to help you put the tablet away.

The next time, call your child's attention to the icons that appear on the screen when it is turned on. Demonstrate how a sound or movement is triggered by just a light finger touch. This introductory step calls upon your child's attending and tracking skills and helps her understand that the tablet's screen is the center of the action. It also helps her see that your finger tap makes something happen. End the work session at this point to build excitement about the next time.

In the next session, invite your child to interact with the screen by touching places you point out to her. Include both auditory and visual responses in this session. The triggered sounds and noises again call on your child's attending and tracking skills, and she will quickly learn that her finger tap can have many effects on this machine.

In subsequent work sessions, continue to demonstrate and invite your child to touch various icons on pre-selected scenes and activities. At this point, your child needs to summon increased attention and employ both fine motor and visual discrimination skills in order to take in the whole screen and spot the special places where a tap causes something to happen. Be sure to end the session while her interest is still high.

As with anything you elect to teach your child, it is wise to always take time to review earlier steps before proceeding to any new aspect you plan to demonstrate. Knowledge and confidence will reduce the possibility of frustration over a forgotten routine or app sequence and increase your child's enjoyment of the tablet. As she becomes familiar with and secure about interacting with the screen, operating the new machine will become second nature as well as a continually interesting challenge.

THE ADULT ROLE

As outlined in the previous section, the way you introduce your young learner to a tablet can have a great impact on her attitude toward the new machine. Presenting the device as a learning tool rather than a toy is crucial; so is building familiarity with the tablet and its activities in a step-by-step manner. Of course, the adult role changes rather than ends once your child is comfortable with the tablet. At this point, your efforts to supervise and share your youngster's work time will continue to pay big dividends.

First, it is important to be selective about the apps to which you give your child access. Limiting the number of activities available to your youngster at any one time and ensuring that they fit her learning needs will avoid wasted money and fruitless teaching time. In addition, you'll reduce the possibility of boredom with an app that's too familiar or too easy. You'll also avoid frustration with an activity that's too hard. You can research app possibilities yourself, confer with other parents about their recommendations, or ask for advice from the professionals involved with your child. Experimenting with a particular app via an online trial, free download, store demo, or a tryout on a friend's tablet can help you feel more confident in your choice. (For more information on choosing apps, see Chapter 7.) It is also suggested that you rotate the apps on your tablet regularly to keep the activities fresh. Doing this eliminates the threats of overuse, boredom, and playing simply for entertainment's sake.

Once your tablet is up and running, it is advisable to establish rules regarding its use. Setting a time limit on work sessions right from the start is a good way to avoid arguments with a child who wants to work longer than you feel is reasonable. You may wish to set a timer, as this can further reduce conflict by implying that the object, rather than you, controls your child's work time. Consider the duration of tablet work sessions carefully, taking into account factors such as your child's age, developmental level, and attention span. Permitting too little time can be frustrating, but allowing too long a work session can blur the line between educational use and entertainment, marring the positive effects of the device. It may be wise to start with a five- or ten-minute session and, if appropriate, increase the length of your child's work sessions in small increments over a period of time. After all, you want to encourage practice and success in building new skills rather than just game-playing.

It's also a good idea to maintain control over the location of your youngster's tablet work. Some parents and teachers choose to eliminate the risks inherent in carrying the device around by having their child use the machine only when it is on its charger. This also keeps the tablet in a central location, making supervision easier. For greater flexibility, you can designate several work areas, such as a desk or the kitchen and dining room tables, and encourage your child to choose her spot each time. Regardless, it is important to designate areas that are off-limits to ensure your child's safety, protect the tablet, and facilitate your monitoring of your youngster's work sessions.

As a supervising adult, you can do a lot to increase your child's success with the apps and activities you provide. Share her work time whenever possible, making helpful observations about onscreen items, asking questions to enhance comprehension, and praising her progress. Of course, if making eye contact or maintaining attention is an area of difficulty for your child, your presence while she works may actually inhibit her progress. If this is the case, you can make simple, positive statements before turning the tablet on, sit quietly while your youngster is working, and observe and praise her again after the machine is powered off.

Either way, your mutual enjoyment of your child's work time will add to the learning experience and help you both to make a connection.

Tempting as it may be to take charge of the tablet's maintenance for efficiency's sake, it can benefit your child to share in the device's upkeep. Learning the procedures for cleaning, charging, and encasing the tablet will pique your child's sense of responsibility and help her continue to appreciate the machine's value, importance, purpose, and relative fragility. In addition, periodic chats about the tablet's upkeep will provide another opportunity for positive communication between you and your youngster.

TABLET ISSUES AND CONCERNS

The surprising fascination young children have with tablet technology has been widely reported, as has the fact that such devices and apps enable improved focus and efficient learning. However, educators and child development professionals have voiced concern that the tremendous pull of interactive media can lead to too much of a good thing. Use of tablet technology by young children is too recent a phenomenon to have triggered specific research about the effects of overuse, but there is certainly no shortage of warnings on the subject.

Wolfram Schultz, a Swedish neuropsychologist, uncovered the fact that dopamine, a feel-good chemical that is closely tied to motivation and learned responses, was released in laboratory monkeys who anticipated and learned to predict rewards from a visual stimulus. This same chemical comes into play at the sight of vivid colors and pictures on a computer screen, rewarding users with rushes of excitement and encouraging them to continue the activity at hand. Dr. Schultz's sobering conclusion has been seconded by London researcher Dr. Paul Grasby, whose team found that dopamine production in the brain doubles during video game play, which is highly similar to interacting with a tablet screen. The rapid-fire visual stimulation brings a sense of euphoria that makes you crave additional play, suggesting that addiction to video-centric interactive devices is a real possibility no matter what the user's age. While tablets and apps are known to have countless educational benefits, particularly for special needs children, too much high-tech exposure is clearly something parents and teachers need to guard against.

The American Board of Pediatrics actually recommends avoiding TV and other entertainment media for children under the age of two, because the rapid brain development that takes place during the early years is best enhanced by interaction with people rather than machines. In addition, many longtime teachers point to the positive influence that talking and reading have on a child's social, language, and reading skills. These educators note an increased tendency for their most tech-savvy students to tune out whole-class instruction and withdraw from group activities that simply can't offer the desired level of stimulation. Here, again, moderation in the use of technology seems to be the key to avoiding this pitfall.

A special needs youngster's individual circumstances may make it necessary to deviate from doctors' general recommendations, however, just as her ability level may prevent her from engaging in standard parent-child play, conversation, or socialization with other children. Physical factors, neurological issues, and attention deficit problems can certainly get in the way of ordinary teaching. If this is the case with your child, you must find other ways to promote playful, positive interaction and exposure to the movement, music, and art (as feasible) that are known to enhance reasoning and thinking. If your child has greater success with learning when a machine is the skill-building agent, you can by all means formulate your own plan for engaging, stimulating, and teaching her—a plan that includes frequent use of tablet technology regardless of her age. By choosing challenging but doable activities and ensuring careful monitoring of your special learner's tablet work, you'll provide a path to success that, despite being unconventional, is absolutely effective.

TABLET DO'S AND DON'TS

The skill-building benefits of tablets and apps to young children have become undeniable. Nevertheless, it is also clear that the overuse of tablets by youngsters can have a distinct downside. To achieve optimal learning conditions, the adult in charge should maintain control of all aspects of a child's tablet work, thereby avoiding the numerous drawbacks of excessive use. What follows is a helpful list of suggestions for getting the most from the time your child spends using this special machine.

Do . . .

❏ ask your child's teacher or therapist to recommend apps that will be beneficial.

❏ be part of your child's work time whenever possible. Be sure to make helpful observations, ask questions that will increase her understanding, and offer lots of praise.

❏ limit the number of icons on the screen to improve focus and prevent your child from getting off course.

❏ cover the machine's volume button with matching tape to make it impossible to blast the sound. If this can't be done, cover the speaker with clear tape to muffle sudden volume increases.

❏ control your child's tablet time by requiring that she get permission before using the device.

Don't . . .

❏ give up control of your child's tablet use by conveying that it is "her machine."

❏ absolve your older child of responsibility by taking on the cleaning and charging of the tablet.

❏ yield to the temptation to let the tablet entertain your child while you tend to chores.

❏ undermine your child's attention skills by allowing tablet use while she is also watching TV.

❏ let your child use the tablet near water, such as in the bathroom or by a pool or kitchen sink.

By blending the guidelines above with some common sense and your unique knowledge of your child, it will be easy to ensure that your family's tablet time builds your parent-child connection, improves your youngster's targeted skills, and is enjoyable for both of you.

CONCLUSION

Tablets and apps have been shown to have great potential for improving the social and learning skills of special needs children. As Chapter 3 has demonstrated, you can set the stage for a successful experience with carefully selected software, a preplanned and gradual introduction to the device and its apps, and a commitment to monitoring and sharing your youngster's work time. Direct involvement in your child's tablet use will pay big dividends by enhancing her comprehension of onscreen activities, her academic development, and—best of all—her interactions with you.

When your child is ready to begin using the tablet on a regular basis, you may suspect that her learning experience would be further enhanced by making modifications or additions to the device. Depending on your child's special needs, embellishments and extras are widely available to improve the tablet's durability, make it more user friendly, and increase the accessibility of its features. Chapter 4 provides information that will help you tailor your tablet to your child's special needs.

4

Adapting and Improving Your Child's Tablet

Eight-year-old Max was diagnosed with attention deficit hyperactivity disorder (ADHD) when he was in kindergarten. Max is affectionately described by his mother as "an accident waiting to happen," and his impulsive, rapid-fire movements make him clumsy, injury-prone, and a tremendous challenge to supervise. Extra short on attention, he likes to explore things with his hands rather than watch or listen to a demonstration that won't hold his focus. However, many items do not fare well with his rough, hasty touch. Max has particularly bad luck with household electronics, having broken the family's desktop computer five times, the TV three times, and the brand new gaming system twice. In addition, he has lost or broken more remote and game controls than his parents can remember.

At the start of the school year, Max's teacher suggested that working on a tablet computer might improve the child's focus and thus give him crucial practice with the math facts and letter sounds that were eluding him in class. Knowing their son's track record with electronic devices, however, Max's parents were uncertain about the wisdom of such an investment. A little research revealed that there were ways to improve the durability of a tablet so that it could withstand their child's rough handling and afford him important access to the device's educational benefits. Max's parents chose to go ahead with the purchase and included some protective features for their machine.

Today, Max is the enthusiastic user of a sturdily encased, well-shielded tablet. In its short lifetime, his machine has been bumped, dropped, knocked off a table, sat on, and splashed with apple juice. However, the tablet remains intact and in good working order because of the safety features his parents so wisely provided. Best of all, Max's daily use of the device is yielding great academic benefits. These days, he automatically adds and subtracts numbers up to ten and is practicing with numbers up to twenty. In addition, the boy's sight-reading vocabulary has more than doubled since he began working on the tablet. A more-confident Max is now an eager volunteer during class lessons.

The recent explosion in tablet use by children quickly revealed a need to protect these pricey machines from mishaps by rough or inexperienced hands. It was no surprise that youngsters could find endless ways to damage these devices, albeit inadvertently, and this knowledge spawned an important market aimed at maximizing tablet durability. In this chapter, you will find helpful information about the types of protective products available for the tablet on which your child works. You'll also get a look at the add-ons that can improve a machine's "child friendliness" by making it easier for little hands to use and even more pleasing to a youngster's eye. Finally, this chapter presents important information about the assistive apparatus that can make tablet use easier for many children with special learning needs. Keep reading to discover new ways to enhance your family's tablet and provide an optimal working experience for your child.

IMPROVING A TABLET'S DURABIITY

Every parent and teacher understands the risks of placing a breakable object in the hands of a child. A youngster's underdeveloped eye-hand coordination, difficulty assessing risks, and tendency toward thoughtless, hasty movements all increase the likelihood of damage to fragile objects. While Max's story at the start of this chapter may be an extreme example of the mishaps that can befall a tablet used by a child, spills, scratches, drops, and the like might be expected in almost any case—even with adult supervision. Nevertheless, countless parents and child development specialists feel that the academic and social gains being shown by young tablet users outweigh the risks to their machines. Therefore, it makes sense to do all you can to safeguard the tablet on which your child will be working.

Of course, it is wise to consider the habits and dexterity of your young user before even making a tablet purchase. Machines vary widely in their ability to absorb impact and withstand assault by moisture or sharp objects, so it pays to do some comparison shopping. Reading product reviews online or in technology magazines can yield valuable input from users of the product you are considering. At the store, don't hesitate to move and lift the machine and work its parts to gauge how it might fare in your child's hands as compared to other models. Some tablet manufacturers have moved toward a textured exterior that reduces the chance that a device will slide during use and also offers a better grip when carried. Other machines, billed as "heavy duty," are decidedly more rugged in construction than conventional tablets; however, these tend to be costly enough to be out of reach for a great many buyers. You may instead wish to consider purchasing protective coverings for a mainstream tablet.

A tablet's screen is certainly its most important feature, but it is also a comparatively fragile component that can be easily damaged. Fortunately, screen-protecting films are widely available to safeguard your machine against smears, dust, scratches, dampness, and fingerprints. These clear protectors adhere directly to the screen and, as a bonus, often help to reduce glare and preserve the brightness of your display. While screen protectors can be a challenge to apply due to the desire for a perfect edge-to-edge fit without bubbles of trapped air, your salesperson can often help you with this task. When your tablet's screen protector begins to show signs of wear, you can peel it off and begin again with a fresh layer of protective film.

A tablet's portability is one of its most attractive attributes. However, carrying the machine from place to place, or even positioning it too near the edge of a table during use, invites the possibility of bumping one of its sides into another fixed object—or worse, having the device fall vertically to the floor. Manufacturers realized early on that encasing the edges of a tablet in an impact-resistant material would offer a line of defense in the event of such mishaps. Protective shells or bands are available to wrap the sides, or the sides and back, of your tablet, providing a shield of molded plastic, rubber, wood, or foam. As the market for such tablet shells grows, some of these protective add-ons are being made with carry handles, side grips, or rippled backs to further safeguard your device against an inadvertent drop.

When tablet computers first soared to popularity, the advisability of covering an idle machine quickly became clear. The earliest tablet covers were dust-sparing envelope-style sleeves with an opening at one end. Cases made of protective foam and with zippered openings, which doubled as impact protection for a machine, soon followed. Carry handles to safeguard against dropping were next, along with multilayered construction for additional padding, snap and velcro closures for easier access, and compartments to hold everything from extra hardware to a pad and pencil. Improvements and innovations to tablet cases continue, and many of today's designs are multifunctional and meant to stay on the machine all the time. These cases continue to function as protective shock absorbers, but many also have strategic openings to the machine's ports and jacks, in addition to the ability to fold back and serve as a tablet stand. Moreover, there has been a veritable explosion in the colors, designs, and variety of materials used in case construction, allowing tablet users to make a fashion statement if desired. All in all, the possibilities for items to protect your tablet are ever-changing and seemingly limitless.

INCREASING THE CHILD-FRIENDLINESS
OF TABLET COMPUTERS

The appeal of a tablet computer to young users has been well established, for the device's nonstop stream of color, light, sound, and action has proven virtually irresistible to children. While this fledgling market segment may have been a surprise at first, manufacturers have been quick to turn their efforts in this direction, rolling out numerous tablets and accessories designed just for the younger set. Some of these items have been designed to make tablets simpler to use, while others have been created strictly for fun and added appeal.

Generally speaking, children are best served by ease of use in any device that is new to them. Of course, mastering the ins and outs of a tablet computer takes time and patience, as does learning to use the apps that are provided. Add to this a parent's or teacher's rules for regulating tablet work time, and it is easy to see the potential for frustration on the part of a child who is learning to use the device. By taking into account a child's small hands, lesser dexterity, shorter attention span, and natural impulsivity, manufacturers are making tablet use easier for youngsters. Machines and add-ons are being designed to override and eliminate these potential roadblocks to a child's success with this technology.

As a means of attracting young tablet users and their parents, the market now offers tablets that have been made strictly for children. These machines tend to be extra-small, lightweight, and less expensive than mainstream tablets, in addition to featuring sturdy construction, brilliant colors, and entertaining designs. Kids-only devices come with preloaded content that can include everything from e-books, learning games, and creative tools to still cameras, camcorders, video players, and webcams. Parental controls are also widely available, and in many cases, these tablets have the ability to sync to a household computer—both to download more apps and to monitor progress on educational activities. These child-friendly machines do have a significant limitation, however. Technically, they are toys rather than computers, and most do not come with Internet browsers. Their built-in Wi-Fi capability exists only for connecting the device to the manufacturer's website. So, while tablets designed for children have a great many advantages, their potential for long-term or more global usage is restricted.

Many tablet buyers therefore choose to provide a regular machine for their child's use, usually arming the device with some of the important protective features previously discussed. In addition to making such well-advised efforts to child-proof your machine, it is easy to find attention-grabbing, child-oriented accessories for your tablet that can make it even more fun to use. The protective cases and bumpers described earlier are sold in a host of appealing colors and patterns, and some are made to resemble animals, popular toys, and cartoon or game characters. The same fun approach is being taken with the design of toy-like tablet stands and character headphones, both geared toward pleasing young tablet users. Wide-barrel, enhanced-grip styluses are available for use with drawing or writing apps, as are wireless wipe-clean keyboards for youngsters who aren't ready to type on a touchscreen. Additionally, you can avoid the frustration of a drained battery by purchasing an external device that provides backup power.

Parents and teachers often find that their youngsters are extra-motivated to work on devices that exhibit a degree of "personality." There are many impermanent but pleasing ways to decorate or personalize your child's machine, from foam stick-on letters to easy-peel decals and pictures. Additionally, there are eye-catching wire organizers available that will be useful if you suspect that the machine's cords and cables present a potential hazard or distraction. Finally, if your youngster uses a tablet while travelling or visiting, you have the option of providing a car-charger adapter to preserve battery life, a car-headrest mount for long rides, a clip-on light to illuminate your child's work area, and a lightweight travel stand for supporting and properly inclining the machine away from home.

As you may suspect, it has been a fairly easy task for manufacturers to cater to and increase children's fascination with tablet computers. First, they considered those characteristics with the potential to grab and hold a youngster's attention—cute faces, say, or bold colors and designs—and used this knowledge to create kids-only tablets as well as embellish and transform mainstream machines. Second, and of equal importance, companies have paid great attention to eliminating roadblocks to a child's physical management of such a device, with add-ons and accessories that ensure ease of use for even the youngest tablet users. Today's child-friendly adaptations and innovations have cleared a path toward improved confidence, increased enjoyment, and additional learning opportunities via tablet technology for children.

ENABLING TABLET USAGE BY SPECIAL NEEDS YOUNGSTERS

As you know, a tablet can provide special needs kids with unprecedented learning opportunities through apps that have been designed to develop and enhance a wide range of skills. Necessary adjustments can be made to any tablet to modify screen brightness, text size, and volume. And for those children who need them, additional enhancements and assistive features are available to cope with specific learning challenges.

A vast amount of software has been created for individuals with physical, social, and academic difficulties. Often designed by child-development professionals, special education teachers, and parent experts, there are activities and games that do everything from side-stepping learning hurdles to teaching social skills to enabling the expression of thoughts and needs. The recognition of the important special-needs market has also led to an expansion of the assistive capabilities built into new tablets. Text-to-speech and word-prediction features, which allow a user to hear what he taps or types and also help with spelling, are often preloaded onto machines, along with voice recognition, vocabulary-building, and augmentative communication software that "speaks" words or phrases designated by the user. Conversely, there are speech-to-text programs that enable a child with limited hand dexterity to create text, send email, search the web, and launch applications on his tablet simply by speaking. A tablet's audio and video recording and playback features give children with writing or language difficulties an alternative means of telling a story, presenting an essay or homework assignment, or simply being creative.

A child who struggles to speak can enjoy social interaction by tapping an icon or image on a tablet screen to express himself. He, his parents, or his teachers can employ software to create storyboards with personal photographs and pre-recorded audio. He can view familiar visual prompts (preselected onscreen pictures that are used as signals) to anticipate new activities, improve his focus, and review or recall social rules, upcoming events, or his daily schedule. A hearing-impaired youngster can communicate with the help of enhanced volume or a keyboard. In addition, he can rely on enhanced video and camera quality for easier lip reading and signing during Skype chats. He can also add external speakers and a microphone to a tablet for better amplification and audio quality, making apps more enjoyable and improving his ability to have conversations online.

Assistive features also exist for children with visual impairments. A tablet's audio capability and text-to-speech software (a program that reads onscreeen print aloud), plus an upgraded visual display and external speakers, can vastly improve a visually impaired child's access to learning activities, pre-recorded verbal prompts and instructions, stories, and even videos. For older children, there are also talking email programs, which, like the text-to-speech software previously mentioned, allow the user to hear his onscreen selections or his own typed words. For learners of Braille, the universal alphabet for the blind, there are tablet keyboards with Braille keys to facilitate writing. In addition, new technology can create a modern eight-key Braille keyboard on a tablet's touchscreen that orients itself to the user's fingertips no matter where they land on the screen.

For youngsters whose progress is impeded by physical problems, developmental challenges, or intellectual delays, there are a host of adaptive devices that can smooth the path to tablet technology and its many learning benefits. Adjustable tablet stands, which hold a device steady and at the desired angle, are available, as are table and wheelchair mounts that serve the same purpose. There are tablet cases with built-in amplifiers and others with shoulder straps to serve children who carry their machines for communication purposes. For youngsters who struggle with finger dexterity, there are large-keyed wireless keyboards, styluses that can be strapped to the hand or head, and special controllers and keyboards that allow a user to hear his onscreen choices. Children who text, but have trouble typing on a touchscreen, can use an oversized wireless keyboard to create their messages. If operating buttons, switches, keys, or a mouse for a tablet poses difficulty, there are numerous adaptive models, cheek- and chin-controlled versions, and still others that can be strapped to the palm with Velcro. There are even eye-tracking devices that employ the user's eye movements to type, tap, and otherwise manage onscreen interactions. (See the inset on page 70.) Finally, there are Home button covers that can offset the tendency to close apps, which interrupts valuable practice. No matter what the roadblock to a child's learning progress, it would seem that help is at hand. Part Two of this book contains information to guide you in this endeavor. (See Chapter 6 for specific product recommendations.)

CONCLUSION

As you have seen in Chapter 4, there are a great many ways to tailor a tablet computer to your child's work habits, maturity level, interests, and developmental capabilities. You can provide safeguards to shield the machine's screen and exterior from everyday mishaps. You can encourage your child's pride and delight in owning and using the device by personalizing and decorating its exterior and accessories. You can furnish add-ons to ensure that your tablet is as easy as possible to use. Finally, you can consider your child's special physical or academic circumstances and provide both devices and software that maximize success in important developmental areas. With manufacturers catering to children, who now represent a large portion of technology users, there is little reason for parents and teachers to fear a poor return on a tablet investment or worry about the fate of a machine in small hands. While the phrase "child-friendly tablet computer" may once have seemed a contradiction in terms, these words make perfect sense today.

CONCLUSION

A Look Ahead

Advancements in technology are rapid-fire and constant, and tablet computers are no exception. Machines and features that were considered state-of-the-art just a year ago have already been replicated and refined, and this trend is expected to continue. Already on the market and evolving quickly are case-battery combinations for prolonged tablet sessions, as well as work surfaces that charge machines while they are still in use. Multi-layer shock-absorbing screen shields and tablet covers—some even billed as "bullet proof"—have been created from polymer combinations that were years in the making and have withstood exhaustive impact testing. The wireless connectivity market is also undergoing rapid change as seen by the recent explosion in tablet owners who choose to optimize Internet access by connecting to multiple carriers.

Recently released and already the subject of significant improvement efforts are hybrid machines that blend the benefits of a tablet with important features of other devices. There are phone-tablet hybrids that enable users to carry and operate just a single machine, as well as laptop-tablet hybrids that offer a rotating, detachable keyboard with its own battery power. In addition, there are oversized tablets that are perfect for group settings or to suit the needs of children with muscle-control issues. Some of these are tabletop models; others are wall-mounted devices. All have multi-user capabilities along with increasingly upgraded touch-screens and accessibility features.

A peek into the world of consumer electronics, provided by publications, trade shows, and many attention-getting information "leaks," gives a glimpse of technological improvements that are yet to come. Innovations in touch interface are under study that will allow users to perform complex tasks via finger tapping, drumming, or rolling onscreen. Mouse emulation, another breakthrough, will enable pointing, clicking, and scrolling simply through in-the-air hand and finger motions. Also reportedly underway are vast improvements in tablet processor potency that will bring tablet graphics, system performance, and power management to previously unimagined heights. Additionally, technology is en route that will maximize tablet memory, data storage, and pixel resolution. No matter how cutting-edge today's newest devices seem to be, it is clear that huge improvements are on the way.

Technology experts foresee an eventual shift in computer design away from user interface—that is, the need to physically launch and operate programs—and toward the "wearing" of devices that will allow you to execute tasks through subtle movements or speech. This upcoming technology has particularly exciting implications for the special needs population. In the meantime, children, their families, and the professionals in their lives are already enjoying tremendous developmental advancements thanks to tablets that have been adapted to fit their requirements. To help you select the best from what is available right now, Part Two serves as a handy buyer's guide by presenting important information about the best tablets, accessories, adaptive devices, and software for youngsters with learning challenges. Read on for a host of tips and product recommendations, as well as valuable websites that can streamline your shopping.

Your Guide to Tablets, Accessories, and Apps

There's no question that a tablet is costly and that its purchase requires careful consideration under any circumstances. If the tablet is to be used by a child, there is an even greater need to do your homework before making a selection. The problem is that tablet shopping has become a complex undertaking due to the vast number and ever-changing variety of choices. Given the proliferation of tablet-related add-ons and apps aimed at the youth market and the secondary focus on children with special learning needs, device and application purchases can be overwhelming to the average consumer. Fortunately, help is at hand.

Part Two of this book was written to serve as a guide to the selection and purchase of tablets, accessories, and apps. Chapter 5 begins with basic tips for tablet shoppers and goes on to present valuable suggestions for choosing the best machine for your child's particular needs. Information is provided on using product reviews, deciding where to shop, and getting the best deal possible. You'll even find the lowdown on possible grants for special needs learners, along with ideas for trying products out before buying them. Following the chapter on tablets, Chapter 6 offers product recommendations for accessories and add-ons that can enhance the tablet experience of your struggling learner. Chapter 7 then presents guidelines for choosing applications, followed by recommendations for apps that have been designed for children with specific learning challenges. There is also a helpful Glossary and a Resources section that lists the top websites and stores to visit when planning your tablet tech purchases.

If you have decided that a computer tablet can help you break through your child's learning difficulties, the following pages are the best place to start your child's tablet adventure.

5

Choosing the Best Tablet
for Children
With Special Needs

The task of locating the perfect tablet for your child requires a good deal of forethought and research. First, you should weigh your youngster's age and fine motor abilities against a tablet's potential fragility. Also try to match your child's special educational needs to the machine and accessories that will best help her over the long term. Budget will play a large part in your potential purchase, perhaps driving you to eliminate certain machines from consideration due to features you feel are unnecessary. The way your child will use the tablet for social contact—everyday communication, video chatting, or emailing, for instance—will provide further direction in the choice of extras. Then, there is the matter of location. Depending on your geographic region, faster Internet connectivity may be a necessity rather than a frill, making some tablets more functional than others. The eventual need for additional apps should also come into play. How much child-appropriate software is available for the tablet you are considering? How can it be acquired, and at what additional cost? Finally, because the experience of actual tablet users is so important, you should consider whether you know of other children who use the target device successfully and without mishap. Would their parents make the same purchase again?

If you are feeling intimidated or overwhelmed by the prospect of selecting a tablet for your special learner, the following discussions should help to guide you through your purchase.

Ten Practical Tips
For Tablet Shoppers

As mentioned above, the acquisition of a tablet for your child can be a tremendous undertaking even for the most technology-savvy adult. As you begin your search for the perfect machine, the following list of suggestions can steer you in the right direction and serve as a step-by-step framework for your buying experience.

1

Research the many terms common to tablet computers before you begin shopping. Learning the difference between iOS, Android, and Windows operating systems; 3G versus 4G mobile technology; or cellular versus Wi-Fi networking will provide the foundation you need to find the best device for your child. By scrutinizing machines' product descriptions and searching the Internet for the meanings of any unfamiliar terms you encounter, you can boost your technology vocabulary immensely. The online glossaries listed on page 124 of the Resources section should provide you with the definitions you need to navigate the world of tablets.

2

Research the most commonly asked questions about tablet computers. Reading the answers to queries posed by other tablet shoppers will increase your understanding of technological terminology and tablet features, making you a more confident consumer. Many computer manufacturers provide

"FAQ" links on their websites for this purpose. Another option is to perform an Internet search for "tablet FAQs" to learn about the features with which you need to become familiar.

3

Know the difference between mainstream tablets and those created and marketed as children's toys. Some of the newer toy tablets have Internet capability, preloaded games, and structural features similar to those of regular tablets. However, most children's machines have less responsive screens, lesser processing power, and pricey cartridge-style software that is ultimately more expensive than downloadable apps. Also, as children's tablets become more sophisticated in design, their once-attractive prices have increased, as well. Finally, it is wise to consider the long-term usefulness of a children's tablet. Even at the highest end of the market, your ability to add important features will likely be limited.

4

Get as much input as you can from informed people who don't have a vested interest in your purchase. The opinion of a fellow consumer, particularly one who is familiar with your family's tablet needs, is likely to be more helpful than that of a store employee who may be pressured to promote certain products at certain times. You can begin by asking friends and coworkers for advice. Also refer to technology publications and consumer guides for the latest product reviews. Several that are accessible online are discussed in the inset "The Ins and Outs of Product Reviews" found on page 58, and are also listed in the Resources section, which begins on page 123. Finally, find customer reviews and ratings for any tablet of interest by typing the manufacturer, model name and number, and the word "reviews" into your Internet search bar.

The Ins and Outs of Product Reviews

While product reviews in general represent one person's opinion, the writers tend to be either professionals in the field under scrutiny or consumers with firsthand experience using the item under consideration. In any case, reading the postings and weighing the advice presented by reviewers will enable you to directly benefit from their product knowledge. It may also prevent you from making a purchase you will come to regret because the chosen machine lacks a crucial feature or is difficult to use.

Product reviews for tablets and apps are easy to find. Manufacturers' own websites usually offer customer reviews for each product, although the absence of truly negative opinions may cause you to wonder whether all submitted reviews are actually posted. A possibly more objective collection of consumer responses can be found on Amazon's website, www.amazon.com, which contains a Tablet Comparison page with links to hundreds of customer reviews per item. This page also allows you to compare the physical size and components of numerous large and small tablets. Other sources of tablet reviews are available online, both on the websites of technology-oriented publications and on specially created tablet review and comparison pages. A visit to these sites can provide helpful pricing information and star ratings, while allowing you to quickly compare numerous features of the machines in your price range. The Resources section of this book provides a list of websites that offer this valuable information. (See page 124.) Tablet shoppers who prefer a more classic and generic source of product reviews, ratings, information, and advice can browse hard copies of such magazines as *Consumer Reports* or *Popular Mechanics,* available at newsstands and in libraries.

With new releases constantly being added to the children's software that's already on the market, it may be wise to also read reviews of the apps you are thinking of purchasing. Be aware that reviews differ from readily available app descriptions in that they draw on the opinions of educational experts and child-rearing professionals, as well as the experiences of parents and tablet-savvy children. Objective information about the educational value, appeal, age-appropriateness, and difficulty level of the most popular apps can be found on numerous software review sites, many of which offer writers' viewpoints and rankings of the "best" or "top ten" apps. Also offered are online trials and information on the availability of free apps. You can find a list of such websites on page 127 of this book's Resources section. In addition, you can refer to parenting publications and their websites for expert advice about apps that are both appealing and educationally sound. *Parents* (www.parents.com) and *Parenting* (www.parenting.com) are two magazines that provide this sort of helpful information.

Of course, many children with learning challenges have developmental requirements that are different from those of the general population, and this can undermine the value of mainstream app reviews. Depending on your child's physical or educational challenges, the websites of nonprofit organizations that support special needs families can be a good source of more applicable feedback. A visit to the organization's home page often reveals a search bar or resources link that will take you to advice that's relevant to your search. In addition, there are a number of app-review websites that focus on educational software for children with learning challenges. Some sites categorize apps according to diagnosis or skill area, and some also offer software previews and free trials, as well as advice about the best "free" apps for various special needs. More detailed information on choosing apps begins on page 79.

5

Establish a reasonable price range and use it as a guideline as you consider various devices. Shopping with a price and your child's strengths and weaknesses in mind will enable you to prioritize, focus on features that will maximize your tablet's user friendliness, and avoid paying extra for elements that are unnecessary or unsuitable. The inset "The Bottom Line on Tablet Specs," found on page 64, presents recommendations that will help you in this regard.

6

Be cautious about buying a used tablet. Money saved on the purchase of a secondhand machine may not be worth the problems you will have if the processing system is outdated and fails to work with current software. You can check a device's specifications by typing the manufacturer, model name, and number into your Internet search bar and scrolling through the results for a product description. Then do a similar search for any software you plan to buy and check whether its system requirements are compatible with the secondhand tablet.

7

Consider all "bargain" tablets carefully. The least-expensive machines may have processors that are too slow to run the latest apps and may also lack social media capability or important durability elements. Accessories and software may be in short supply for these low-end devices, and your ability to add performance upgrades may be very limited.

8

Watch product demonstrations for information on ease of use. You can ask a friend to show you the features of his or her device, request a demo in your favorite electronics store, or do an online search of model names and numbers for the manufacturers' own how-to videos. In addition, by doing a product search on YouTube (www.YouTube.com) for videos shared by tablet owners, you may be able to find important information about the pros and cons of different machines.

9

Check the extent of app availability for any tablets you consider. It's important to know that some devices will run only the software from the manufacturer's own app store. If you are thinking of buying this type of machine, study the store's offerings online to determine whether the software collection suits your child's educational needs. The web addresses of popular online app stores are included in the Resources section beginning on page 126.

10

Compare prices. Once you have decided on the tablet you wish to buy, investing a little more time in price-shopping is a wise move. Visit comparison-shopping websites, which find and list the wholesalers and retailers currently charging the lowest prices for particular products. On these sites, you'll find links to the sellers' own websites. Additional information about price-shopping websites, as well as other advice on cutting costs, can be found in the section "Money-Saving Tips for Tablet Shoppers" on page 66.

Once you have followed the ten steps detailed above, given consideration to your child's particular needs, and taken time to compare the features of tablets in your price range, you will be ready to make your purchase. Combining knowledge of your child with information about available technology and the complex world of tablet components is the key to choosing your device with confidence.

WHAT TO LOOK FOR IN A TABLET

Apple's iPads have long been the top-selling tablet computer, and their incomparable selection of apps helps to keep the brand in the market's forefront. However, Apple faces sharply increasing competition as less costly Android and Windows devices improve and multiply in number. With tablet prices currently ranging from under $100 to more than $900, and with an incredible variation in design and components available in these machines, how do you decide which device to buy?

As mentioned often in these pages, your child's special needs should be your starting point. A tablet's sturdiness is a primary concern with any young user, of course, but your child's physical or emotional challenges may well translate into even greater wear and tear, as well as a higher incidence of mishaps. Therefore, your device's ruggedness should be a critical consideration. (Helpful information about increasing tablet durability can be found on page 42 of Chapter 4.) Your child's finger dexterity should be another key factor in choosing a machine. Is she able to interact with a small device, or might a 10-inch screen, oversized mouse, chunky stylus, or enlarged keyboard be a better fit? Will your youngster use the tablet to communicate and therefore need it to be lightweight and wearable? If a special stand or supplemental battery is needed, for which tablets are these available? Will your child benefit from text-to-speech and word-prediction features, and are these preloaded in the devices you are considering? Finally, there is the matter of apps to encourage developmental progress. With so many programs available to enhance a tablet's assistive powers, it pays to ask your child's teachers or therapists for advice about machines that are preloaded with apps that will fit her learning needs.

A second focus should be on getting the most for your tablet dollar. Achieving this sometimes means sacrificing unnecessary features to acquire those that will be most helpful to your child—saying "No" to maximized storage capacity, for instance, in order to include a video camera. Keep an eye on your ability to add desired upgrades down the line, as tablets vary widely in their preloaded and add-able content. Product specifications and customer reviews can help you in this regard. (See "The Ins and Outs of Product Reviews" on page 58.) Another area of consideration is Internet connectivity. If online access is a priority for your child, the possibilities may vary according to where you live. Friends, retailers, and your cellular service provider can help you decide whether a tablet with built-in Wi-Fi or 4G capability will cost less in the long run than paying for a monthly data plan. Other key features to weigh during your product search include processor and charging speed. In both cases, you can minimize frustration during your child's work time by investing in the greatest capacities your budget allows. The same is true of battery life, especially if the tablet will accompany your child away from home on a regular basis. A list of desirable specifications for child-friendly tablets is provided in the inset "The Bottom Line on Tablet Specs" on page 64.

Next, you should investigate whether a tablet can be expanded as your child grows. The machine with the longest useful life is certainly going to be the most practical to purchase, so it pays to look beyond, say, the language apps your youngster may need now to the video-making or social media capability that will become important in a few years. For example, if a necessary video camera or speech-to-text program isn't currently present, can it be added later? Can connectivity be upgraded when your child begins to surf the Internet and email friends and family? Perhaps most important, is the range of applications available in a manufacturer's app store large and varied enough to grow along with your child's changing interests and abilities? The addresses of popular app stores can be found on page 126 of the Resources section to help you make this determination.

Finally, it is important to choose your tablet brand wisely. A manufacturer's reputation counts for a great deal, especially if you

The Bottom Line on Tablet Specs

As mentioned previously, the tablet market has exploded with options, bringing an ever-wider range of machine prices and capabilities. While family budgets and children's academic profiles certainly differ, particular features can minimize frustration and maximize enjoyment for your young tablet user. If possible, therefore, look for a device with the specifications set forth in the guidelines below. Keep in mind, of course, that the technology world's nonstop evolution brings continual improvement to tablet components. Always check the manufacturer's website for newly available upgrades.

SCREEN SIZE. The most desirable screen size depends on your child's visual motor and fine motor abilities. A 7- or 8-inch screen translates to a smaller, lighter device and works well for youngsters with good dexterity and vision. Other children may need a 10-inch screen in order to avoid frustration.

SCREEN DISPLAY. The greater the number of pixels—dots that combine to form an image—the sharper and clearer the screen display. For 7- and 8-inch screens, aim for 1,280 x 800 pixels or better. For larger screens, at least 1,920 x 1,080 pixels are recommended.

WEIGHT. Tablets are designed to be portable, and for a child, a lighter-weight device is most manageable. Look for a tablet with a weight of 1.25 pounds or less.

BATTERY LIFE. There are many supplemental battery and charging options available, but if your child will use the device away from home or for communication purposes, a tablet with its

should ever encounter a problem with your machine. The best-known companies are the most likely to stand behind their products, and buying a so-called "name brand" can help you proceed with the greatest confidence. Three of the best-known companies, own long battery life is the easiest way to go. A seven-hour minimum of battery life is recommended.

PROCESSOR SPEED. A larger number of Ghz (gigahertz, or processing speed) will translate into faster tablet performance. Aim for a device with a speed of at least 1.3 Ghz.

RAM (RANDOM ACCESS MEMORY). A device's RAM is a data storage module that allows fast access to the computer's operating system and application programs. RAM is measured in gigabytes (GB), with a larger number of gigabytes indicating faster machine performance. Try for at least 2 GB of RAM.

DUAL CAMERAS. Some tablets lack cameras, and others have only a front-facing camera. Look for a tablet that has both front and rear cameras, which provide access to still photography, photo editing, video making, self-photography, and video chatting.

SPECIAL NEEDS SOFTWARE. Would your child benefit from using a text-to-speech, speech-recognition, communication, or word-prediction program? Depending on her needs, look for a tablet with the necessary programs preloaded or accessible via its app store.

PARENTAL CONTROLS. The ability to set usage, browsing, and downloading limits helps protect a tablet and keeps you in charge of your child's work time. Look for a device with pre-existing control settings or access to a parental control app.

Following the spec guidelines above will help you to acquire a tablet that your child will enjoy and benefit from over the long term.

Apple, Google, and Microsoft, happen to be both developers and manufacturers. All three build their own operating systems, or platforms, with Google and Microsoft also marketing theirs to other tablet manufacturers. Among this second group are prominent companies such as Samsung, Hewlett Packard (HP), and Asus, all of whom offer lines of tablets. Amazon, both an online retailer and a manufacturer of the Kindle product line, is another leader in the tablet market.

Keeping your child's abilities and needs in mind will help you itemize exactly what you are looking for in a tablet and ultimately obtain the most useful elements available within your price range. Once you have determined which manufacturers have reputations that satisfy you, offer suitable tablet capabilities, and provide access to the content your child will need both now and later, you will have become the most educated of tablet customers. At that point, you will be ready for the final aspect of your search—ensuring that you are paying the lowest possible price for your chosen device.

MONEY-SAVING TIPS FOR TABLET SHOPPERS

With tablet prices hovering in the hundreds of dollars and app costs tending to add up quickly, most shoppers are eager for price-cutting ideas. When you have decided on the tablet you desire, there are a number of places to go for potential savings. Naturally, you can watch for sales at local electronics stores, paying particular attention during late summer and early fall, when retailers often try to move out last year's models. You'll also save shipping costs by buying in person. Online retailers such as Amazon (www.amazon.com) often have "Outlet" links on their home pages that can lead you to product markdowns stemming from closeout or overstock situations. You may also find items that were returned or warehouse-damaged but have been refurbished and are sold with a guarantee. Sometimes, low- or no-cost shipping is even available through membership programs or shipping "specials." Most tablet manufacturers' own websites also have "Sale" or "Clearance" links that you can check.

Price-comparison search websites such as Shopping.com (www.shopping.com), Shopzilla (www.shopzilla.com), and Nextag (www.nextag.com) are an excellent way to find items you want at the lowest cost. Simply type the tablet's name and model number into the website's search bar, and you'll be presented with the prices currently being charged for the device by numerous stores and online retailers. Coupon sites may also help save you money. Most sites' home pages provide a search bar or "Electronics" link that will take you to current coupons and discount codes from manufacturers and retailers. Retail Me Not (www.retailmenot.com) and Coupon Cabin (www.couponcabin.com) are examples of coupon sites that do not involve a membership fee.

After researching these money-saving opportunities, you may find that purchasing a tablet computer for your child's use is still beyond your means. If this is the case, there are several avenues to follow for help. First, ask your insurance company whether a tablet might be covered under your policy's Durable Medical Equipment section. Be prepared to state specific reasons why your child is in need of this device. Next, you may wish to ask your school district to provide a tablet, again spelling out the details of her learning needs that make this device crucial. Also, consider approaching local service organizations such as the Rotary Club, Junior League, or Lions Club for financial assistance. With knowledge of your child's learning challenges and information on the ways tablet access can inspire growth, these community leaders might consider making a donation toward the purchase price. There are also a number of organizations that offer funding to assist families of children with special needs. You may wish to apply to one of these foundations, listed on page 130 of the Resources section, for a grant to cover some or all of the cost of a tablet for your child.

As you research different means of financial support, you may be tempted to follow up on online advertisements for tablets that are "free" in return for your performance of a service. Such offers often promise that you can keep a machine after trying it and testing it for a certain period of time. While these arrangements are occasionally legitimate, the completion of product surveys and the sharing of friends' names as potential testers are usually part of the deal. This can lead to personal information being forwarded to other companies, for which the tablet distributor receives payment. Be sure to read the offer's fine print.

Lastly, you can consider undertaking your own fundraising campaign. While you may feel that soliciting donations from friends and relatives is an uncomfortable and inefficient way of raising money for educational technology, online fundraising campaigns are becoming both commonplace and effective. Using fundraising agents such as GoFundMe (www.gofundme. com), Kickstarter (www.kickstarter.com), or ImRaising (www. imraising.com), you can place a live donation tracker on a web page where visitors can read your child's story and choose to contribute.

As you can see, numerous opportunities exist for obtaining financial help so that the best tablet for your child becomes as affordable as it is useful.

6

Choosing the Best
Add-Ons and Accessories
for Children With
Special Needs

There are thousands of add-ons and adaptive items available to enhance the tablet experience of a struggling learner. Special keyboards and mice have been designed for children who find touchscreens difficult to use, adaptive styluses allow learners with fine motor challenges to write and draw with greater ease, straps and mounts give all youngsters easy access to their tablets, and tablet cases protect delicate machinery against drops, bumps, and splatters. There is even technology that enables control of onscreen interactions through the tablet user's eye movements. (See the inset on page 70.) Your child's unique set of strengths and weaknesses will guide you in choosing the accessories that will be most beneficial to him.

The items that follow, while not right for every child, are helpful high-quality favorites of parents and teachers. Be aware that you may sometimes find lower prices by searching for these devices at online retailers and cost-comparison websites. You may also encounter just-released updated models on the website of an item's manufacturer.

Eye-Tracking Devices

Eye-tracking technology, which allows hands-free computer use via built-in cameras, is no longer in its infancy. Available until just recently only for desktop computers, tiny cameras locate the user's eye position and utilize eye movements to create and control onscreen interaction. Understandably, the earliest eye-tracking devices were extraordinarily expensive; but this exciting technology provided computer access to people with motor and communication limitations who could not use their hands to operate a keyboard or mouse, nor their voices to activate assistive software.

As with all technology, tremendous progress is being made in the eye tracking arena, and development now extends to tablets. The Tobii PCEye Go eye tracker, by Tobii Assistive Technology Inc., currently costs $1,995 and works with Windows 8 Pro tablets to enable hands-free control. A device by The Eye Tribe, costing just $99, is being marketed only to developers to increase the potential for eye-controlled apps and games. The Eye Tribe Tracker plugs into the Microsoft Surface tablet with a USB connector and allows eye-controlled login, swiping, typing, and Internet navigation. Trackers for Android and iOS devices are in development. Similarly, a company called Visual Interaction is marketing eye-tracking products to developers as well as research institutes. VI's myGaze products begin at $890 for the Developer Edition, which works with Windows operating systems and a USB connection.

Innovations in eye-tracking technology will continue to simplify tablet use by people with physical and communication challenges, and the general population is likely to join them very soon. It is easy to anticipate an eye-controlled tablet for use in schools, stores, or offices. Eye-controlled TVs are already available, and surely, eye-controlled smartphones will not be far behind!

PRODUCT RECOMMENDATIONS

Each of the entries in the following listings begins by stating the product's name, the manufacturer, and the manufacturer's or distributor's website from which it can be ordered. The listing then offers a brief description of the product, followed by its price. Finally, you'll learn the specific benefit this add-on provides for the special needs child.

KEYBOARDS

VisionBoard2 Large Key Keyboard

Chester Creek Technologies, www.chestercreek.com
This USB-enabled keyboard has oversized, high-contrast black-on-white or black-on-yellow keys. **Price: $85 and up.**

Benefit: This oversized keyboard can assist children with low vision or fine motor difficulties who struggle to use an onscreen keyboard and might have problems with standard-sized, lower-contrast keys.

Wireless Solar Keyboard

Logitech, www.logitech.com
This keyboard is powered by lamps, overhead lighting, or the sun and works for three months on a full charge. Available for iPad, Android, and Windows tablets, this line of wireless keyboards works on Bluetooth technology. **Price: $89.99.**

Benefit: The concave key design of Logitech's keyboard can enable a child who has fine motor delays to type more easily than he could if he were using a two-dimensional onscreen keyboard.

ZAGGKeys Flex

ZAGG Inc., www.zagg.com
The ZAGGKeys Flex wireless, rechargeable keyboard is compatible with both iPad and Android tablets, and provides months of use between charges. Its fold-up case can double as a tablet stand. **Price: $80.00**

Benefit: This lightweight keyboard responds well to both light and heavy touches and can help children who lack the dexterity to use an onscreen keyboard.

STYLUS PENS

HHI Aluminum Stylus Pen

HandHelditems, www.handhelditems.com
This wide-width stylus is made of aluminum and has high sensitivity, which can help children draw and write easily on touchscreens. **Price: $6.95.**

Benefit: The pencil-like construction of this stylus encourages a correct grip and adds authenticity to the practice of letter and number formation.

iPad Steady Stylus Mini

shapedad on Etsy, www.etsy.com/shop/shapedad
This T-shaped stylus is made of durable plastic and aluminum with a conductive fabric tip. It works on all tablets. **Price: $20.00.**

Benefit: The Steady Stylus can be helpful to children who have difficulty holding a pencil but can grasp objects firmly using the whole hand.

iPad Strap Stylus

shapedad on Etsy, www.etsy.com/shop/shapedad
This 8-inch aluminum stylus has a conductive tip and a Velcro hand strap for grip assistance. **Price: $38.00.**

Benefit: By holding the stylus in place so it moves along with the child's hand, this item can help children with limited hand and finger dexterity to write or draw.

TABLET CASES

Defender Series Tablet Cases

OtterBox, www.otterbox.com
These rigorously tested, shock-absorbing cases for iPad and Android tablets include three layers of impact protection. The Defender Series also has sturdy, built-in, full-view screen shields and port covers that guard against dust and dirt. **Price: $79.95 and up.**

Benefit: This item protects a child's tablet against drops and bumps while protecting the screen and ports from dirt and grime.

E-Series and I-Series Waterproof Tablet Cases

Cascade Designs, www.cascadedesigns.com
These rugged zipper-lock waterproofing cases have high-clarity windows that enable the use of touchscreens, cameras, and audio functions. They come in sizes to fit any tablet. **Price: $29.95 and up.**

Benefit: These cases give a child access to all tablet functions while providing protection against rain, splatters, spills, and submersion in water.

SAFEKIDS Children Proof Durable Cases

KHOMO, www.khomoaccessories.com
This line of tablet cases is constructed with dense, heavy-duty foam that covers the tablet's back and sides and extends above the screen surface. The case design exposes buttons and ports, and the sturdy carry handle folds back to serve as a stand. **Price: $19.95.**

Benefit: The SAFEKIDS case provides a handle for safely transporting or propping up a tablet and protects the machine from scratches if a child lays the device face down or drops it.

TABLET STANDS AND MOUNTS

Adjustable Tablet Holders

R.J. Cooper, www.rjcooper.com
This line of tablet holders comes in three sizes: standard adjustable, tall adjustable, and tall/wide adjustable. The holders can be modified to accommodate any tablet with or without a case and can be angled as desired in both landscape and portrait modes. Hardware is included for attaching the holder to an existing positioning arm. **Price: $59.00.**

Benefit: This holder can benefit children with motor delays by keeping the tablet in the desired position during use.

iPad/Tablet Combo Stand

R.J. Cooper, www.rjcooper.com
This dual tray stand holds both a tablet and an accessory keyboard at a steep angle. The adjustable trays are connected by strong Velcro and have rubber bumpers on the bottom. The Combo Stand can hold any tablet with or without a case, and any keyboard with or without a key guard overlay. **Price: $99.00.**

Benefit: By maintaining a steep angle, R.J. Cooper's Combo Stand helps keep the user's eyes looking forward. The position of the tablet and keyboard can be extremely beneficial to children who type with one finger and need to look at the keyboard to locate keys.

Tablet Mounts

R.J. Cooper, www.rjcooper.com
These arm-like mounts include a clamp for attaching to tables, desks, wheelchairs, or bedrails, and also include one of the Adjustable Tablet Holders described on page 74. Four sizes are available, ranging from a three-inch to a twenty-four-inch reach. The mounts can be set in any position and locked in place for firmness. **Price: $119.00 and up.**

Benefit: These mounts can facilitate tablet use for children of any size who work from an adapted desk, wheelchair, or bed.

TABLET STRAPS

GoPad

GoPad, www.gopad.ca
This wearable device, which comes in mini and maxi sizes to fit all tablets, has a neck strap and attached three-position aluminum swing-arm. The GoPad fastens to a tablet and has multiple uses. **Price: $89.00.**

Benefit: Highly versatile, the GoPad can serve as a wall-hanger, desktop stand, or abdominal brace, depending on a child's specific needs as well as his changing circumstances throughout the day.

iPad Tablet Neck Strap

LapWorks, www.laptopdesk.net
This neck strap provides hands-free support for an iPad and many other tablets. The one-inch-wide polyester strap disconnects easily and can also be worn over the shoulder. **Price: $19.95.**

Benefit: This strap allows a child to move about freely while her tablet hangs securely by her side.

Tablet Handler Strap

LapWorks, www.laptopdesk.net
This one-piece adjustable Velcro strap fits all sizes of tablets, enabling a child to slide her hand in and hold the tablet without the stress of gripping it. The strap's hub rotates 360 degrees to allow for portrait or landscape screen viewing. **Price: $39.95.**

Benefit: This strap can prevent dropping mishaps as well as hand fatigue in children who carry their tablets with them for communication.

MICE

BIGtrack Trackball

Infogrip, www.infogrip.com
This oversized, ruggedly built three-inch trackball plugs into a tablet's USB port. Large buttons located behind the trackball help avoid unwanted clicks. **Price $79.00.**

Benefit: The BIGtrack Trackball can help children who struggle with a tablet screen or standard mouse due to poor motor control.

Chester Mouse

Chester Creek Technologies, www.chestercreek.com
This small single-button mouse fits a child's hand and is constructed without a scroll wheel. It benefits youngsters who have difficulty using a tablet touchscreen. **Price: $22.95.**

Benefit: This mouse reduces left-right confusion and helps children who struggle to use a standard mouse's scroll wheel.

Mouse Button-Box

R. J. Cooper, www.rjcooper.com
This 8.5 by 5-inch USB mouse has its buttons located on the left or right as needed, and includes single and left/right click options. The Button-Box can also be used as a foot mouse. **Price: $99.00.**

Benefit: Children with fine motor or eye-hand control difficulties are likely to find this mouse helpful.

HOME BUTTON COVERS

BubCap Ultra

Paper Clip Robot, www.bubcap.com
This adhesive-backed button cover for iPads prevents young children from activating a tablet's Home button but allows adults to press through the cover with a firm touch. BubCap Max, which requires even firmer pressure to activate the covered Home button, is available for use with older, stronger children. **Price: $5.99 per 4-pack.**

Benefit: These protective covers help keep children from accidentally or willfully exiting apps in the middle of an activity.

7

Choosing the Best Apps for Children With Special Needs

For children who have communication or academic delays, physical challenges, or difficulty sustaining attention, learning can be a problem. Now that apps have shown the potential to close these developmental gaps, many youngsters have the opportunity to develop skills with greater success than ever before. The key lies not only in choosing an appropriate tablet and the right add-ons, as described in Chapters 5 and 6, but also in purchasing the best programs for each child. This section begins by discussing the most important factors to look for when selecting apps. It then provides a skill-by-skill listing of applications that have been recommended by parents and professionals who work with special needs children.

GETTING STARTED

With so many apps available and new ones being developed every day, parents seeking help for their special needs child are faced with a potentially overwhelming number of choices. As you start your search for the most appropriate programs, the following list of suggestions—many of which are explored in greater detail in the following pages—can help guide you to the best that technology has to offer your youngster.

Ten Practical Tips
For App Shoppers

1

Once you have focused on the area that you want to develop, such as reading or fine motor skills, ask your child's teachers and therapists for specific recommendations based on not only their knowledge of the apps but also their familiarity with your little learner.

2

Make sure that the app focuses on skill-building rather than just game-playing. Educational apps feature a great deal of interaction that *teaches* your child as she plays.

3

Remember that in addition to stimulating skill development, apps have to be engaging and fun. Look for appealing graphics and programs that either offer your child familiar characters and activities, or can be personalized with photos and names.

4

Look for apps that merge your child's learning style and strengths with her area of weakness.

5

Search for an app with built-in feedback that rewards skill-building.

6

Determine if you can easily share the app with your child to enhance her learning, and if there are real-world activities that you can use to continue the learning experience when your child's work time is over.

7

Make sure that the app doesn't include heavy marketing of related items or another version of the activity

8

Determine if the app is compatible with your tablet.

9

Make sure that the app suits your child's temperament and level of development so that it proves challenging rather than frustrating.

10

Before making a purchase, sample the app by trying a free or "lite" version, by using a friend's copy, or by watching an online demonstration video.

WHAT TO LOOK FOR IN AN APP

Selecting an app is a challenge when the purpose is not to entertain your child but to help her develop academically, socially, or emotionally. Although most tablet applications are relatively inexpensive, you want to avoid wasting your youngster's work time with programs that are inappropriate or ineffective. The following discussion should help.

Every app you get for your child, should, first of all, target a specific skill. That's why your first task is to clearly identity the skill or skills you want your child to practice. But since your youngster won't gain any benefit from the application unless she uses it frequently, it also must engage her attention. One of the best ways to do this is to choose apps with her learning style in mind. For instance, if your child is a visual learner, she will probably be drawn to activites that provide onscreen prompts in addition to audio instructions.

If she is more attuned to auditory stimulation, be sure the app you choose contains plenty of music, sounds, and conversation. Be aware that in an effort to appeal to all learning styles, many mainstream apps are designed to tap *many* senses. This may offer exactly the kind of activity needed to hold your young learner's attention as she improves the target skill. On the other hand, this multisensory approach may be too stimulating for your child. Only you know for sure. If you feel that your youngster doesn't do well when faced by many different types of stimuli, choose programs that emphasize the specific kind of stimulation that seems to be most appealing to her. Often, an effective app successfully merges your child's area of difficulty with her learning strength. For instance, a child who has word-finding difficulty but a love for visual stimuli may benefit from an activity that announces the names of objects as your child turns cards in an attempt to make matches.

Another good way to engage a child is to choose an educational app that includes her favorite characters and activities, or one that can be personalized with photographs, familiar names, and preferred activities. These approaches are likely to capture and hold your child's attention while she learns. An engaging app should also be highly responsive and include colorful, appealing graphics that are large enough to be navigated by little hands. The app should be easy to use, with a short introduction and clear, simple rules that allow a child to work without frequent assistance. It should also have built-in-feedback, as a child who is rewarded for her progress will experience greater confidence and staying power.

It is important to check the app's recommended age range as specified by the manufacturer, as this will give you some idea of the skill level required by the program. However, your child's developmental level is just as important. In the end, your knowledge of your youngster's unique abilities and temperament is your most valuable resource. The app should challenge and engage your child without causing confusion or frustration. Ideally, it will also contain multiple settings so that you can match the difficulty level to your youngster's current stage of learning.

You will probably find it difficult to get app recommendations from doctors or other professionals who do not know your child. Experts recognize that no two children are alike in regard to developmental pace and learning needs, so they are usually reluctant to make blanket suggestions. But once you have decided on the goal of your child's work time—say, enhancing communication skills—consider asking your child's teachers and therapists for specific suggestions. Special needs resource websites, such as those found on page 128 of the Resources section, are another great source of comprehensive and up-to-date listings, descriptions, and reviews of special needs apps. Some sites group app titles by skill area, which is a very helpful feature.

In the end, you will feel most confident about the apps you purchase if you take a few steps to ensure their suitability for your child. First, consider having your child try out the free or "lite" version of the app, if one is available. If you see that your child likes and succeeds with the activity, you will feel better about paying for the app's full version. To view a demonstration of how the app works, you can also click the app store's YouTube link, if present, or search YouTube.com on your own. Additionally, it is wise to check the designer's website for support information, in case you encounter a problem with your purchase. As a final step, you can use your advance knowledge of any educational app to decide whether it measures up to the standards presented in the inset "Setting the Bar for Educational Apps," found on page 84.

Setting the Bar for Educational Apps

It can be hard to determine which of the many thousands of advertised "educational apps" will actually *teach* your child, as opposed to simply presenting information without regard to outcome. To help in your search, apply the statements below to any app you are considering, using a ranking from 0 (Never) to 5 (Always).

❑ The app allows you to easily change settings to match your child's specific learning needs.

Rating: _____

❑ Your child will quickly be able to launch and interact with all phases of the app without adult assistance.

Rating: _____

❑ The activity seems stimulating and challenging enough to encourage long-term interest.

Rating: _____

❑ The app's provided skill practice takes place in real-life situations—a school or store setting, for instance—rather than through game-playing.

Rating: _____

❑ Work generated by your child can be easily printed, displayed, and, if appropriate, shared via social media to encourage pride in her progress and accomplishments.

Rating: _____

❑ The app has built-in rewards that inspire extra practice and skill improvement.

Rating: _____

❑ The app collects information on your child's performance that both you and she can review.

Rating: _____

If your total ranking falls between 25 and 35, you can feel confident that the app under consideration makes the grade as an educational tool.

PRODUCT RECOMMENDATIONS FOR APPS

The educational apps described on pages 90 to 110 are among the best available according to parents, teachers, and therapists who work with special needs children. While these programs have been divided into categories based on the targeted learning skill, it is important to be aware many educational apps can spur development in more than one skill area. Ultimately, it may pay to review each of the app descriptions. To assist you in homing in on the apps that can offer your child the greatest benefits, the table that begins on page 86 alphabetically lists the programs recommended in this book and indicates the areas that are likely to improve from the use of each one.

Each of the entries in the following listings begins by stating the application's name, the suggested user's age range, the manufacturer, and the website from which the app can be ordered. It then offers a brief description of the product, followed by the price and the specific benefits it was designed to provide for the special needs child. Finally, you'll find the type of tablet—iPad, Android, and/or Windows—with which the program is compatible. If an app of interest is not compatible with your tablet, bear in mind that popular programs designed for one line of machines are often released at a later time for other devices. The tablets referenced at the bottom of each entry are currently accurate, but because technology is ever-changing, it makes sense to check the listed website to see if that app has become available for your child's machine. Be aware, too, that the websites that offer apps can change over time, so if you can't find the program you want on the listed site—or if that site no longer exists—you may be able to locate it through your favorite search engine.

Although each of the recommended programs has proven helpful to many children, every child's needs and responses are unique. If a chosen application fails to engage your child or to help him learn the targeted skill, don't be afraid to try another app. You are the best judge of what works for your child.

MATCHING UP APPLICATIONS WITH SKILL AREAS

Name of App	Organization and Scheduling	Social Learning	Speech and Communication
abc PocketPhonics (page 103)			
Action Sight Words Games (page 103)			
AutismXpress (page 96)		■	
Baby Sign and Learn (page 97)			■
Balloonimals (page 101)			
Bluster! (page 104)			
Bubbles (page 99)			
BugMath (page 108)			
Calm Counter (page 92)		■	
Choiceworks (page 90)	■	■	
Danny the Dragon Meets Jimmy (page 97)			
Dexteria (page 99)			
Dot to Dot Numbers and Letters (page 99)			
DragonBox Algebra 5+ (page 108)			
Drawing Pad (page 100)			
EDA Play (page 101)			
Elmo Loves 123s (page 109)			
First Words With Phonics (page 104)			■
First-Then Visual Schedule HD (page 90)	■		
Gabby Tabs—AAC for Kids (page 94)			■
HOPE Words (page 98)			■
How Would You Feel If . . . (page 92)		■	■
iCommunicate (page 94)			
iPractice Verbs (page 95)			■
iReward Chart (page 90)	■		
iWriteWords (page 106)			
Knee Bouncers Big Little Games (page 102)			

Hearing Impairment	Fine Motor Skills	Visual Impairment	Reading	Writing	Math
	■		■	■	
			■		
■					
■					
	■	■			
			■		
	■				
					■
■					
	■				
	■		■		■
					■
	■				
	■	■			
					■
■			■		
■					
	■		■	■	
	■	■			

MATCHING UP APPLICATIONS WITH SKILL AREAS

Name of App	Organization and Scheduling	Social Learning	Speech and Communication
LetterSchool (page 106)			
Marble Math (page 109)			
Marble Math Junior (page 109)			
Model Me Going Places (page 93)		▓	
My DPS (page 93)		▓	
My Talking Picture Board (page 102)			
myHomework (page 91)			▓
Old MacDonald HD (page 98)			▓
Peekaboo Barn (page 102)			
PictoPie Education (page 91)	▓		
Proloquo2Go (page 95)			▓
Rainbow Sentences (page 96)			▓
Scout's 123 Carnival (page 110)			
Sensory Light Box (page 103)			
Sentence Builder (page 106)			
Share My ABCs (page 107)			
Social Adventures (page 93)		▓	
Speech Therapy for Apraxia—Words (page 96)			▓
Storybook Maker (page 107)			
SUPER WHY! (page 105)			
Time Timer (page 91)	▓		
Touch and Learn—Emotions (page 94)		▓	
Uncolor Dogs (page 100)			
Wet-Dry-Try Suite (page 108)			
What's That Sound? (page 98)			
Wheels on the Bus (page 101)			▓
Word Magic (page 105)			
YodelOh Math Mountain (page 110)			

Hearing Impairment	Fine Motor Skills	Visual Impairment	Reading	Writing	Math
	■			■	■
	■				■
	■				■
		■			
■					
■					
	■	■			
	■				■
	■	■			
			■	■	
	■	■		■	
				■	
			■	■	
	■				
				■	
■					
	■				
			■		
					■

ORGANIZATION AND SCHEDULING APPS

Choiceworks (for ages 4 and up)

Bee Visual, LLC, www.beevisual.com
This picture-based app has three boards—Daily Schedule, Waiting, and Feelings—with accompanying books. Each board reinforces expected behaviors and can be set with pictures from a library or a child's own images. Audio can be added to further personalize the activities. **Price: $6.99.**

Benefit: This app teaches the need for and encourages task completion, waiting and turn-taking, and understanding and expressing feelings. Currently for iPad devices.

First-Then Visual Schedule HD (for ages 5 and up)

Good Karma Applications, www.goodkarmaapplications.com
This app enables the creation of customized visual schedules showing daily events or steps needed to complete a particular activity. A child's own photos and voice can be added to this comforting overview, and multiple schedules can be created and saved. The app offers a choice of full-screen, side-by-side, or list formats. **Price: $9.99.**

Benefit: This app provides positive behavior support for children with developmental or communication delays that make it a challenge to complete or transition between activities.
Currently for iPad and Android devices.

iReward Chart (for ages 3 and up)

iReward Chart, www.iRewardChart.com
This app provides an ongoing visual record of a child's earned rewards for desired behaviors, task completion, and meeting abstract goals such as "waiting patiently." A task and reward are selected, and the child's progress toward task completion is tracked and shown onscreen. **Price: $4.99.**

Benefit: The chart's continual display of rewards in progress and rewards earned can increase a youngster's motivation, productivity, and adherence to rules and routines.
Currently for iPad and Android devices.

myHomework (for ages 9 and up)

instin, LLC, https://myhomeworkapp.com
This app for students has a colorful calendar display to help a child stay organized and manage school responsibilities. Be aware that although this app is free, it contains ads for a myHomework account, which, for $1.99, provides assignment reminders and syncs to teachers' class pages. **Price: Free.**

Benefit: This app helps a child keep track of her daily schedule, along with schoolwork, homework assignments, and upcoming tests.
Currently for iPad, Android, and Windows 8.1 devices.

PictoPie Education (for ages 2 and up)

The App Train/Distant Train, www.pictopie.com
This visual activity board uses drag-and-drop pictures to help children see what is in store for them. A timer portrays how much time remains in the current activity, and a two-minute warning prepares the child for coming events. **Price: $1.99.**

Benefit: This app can help a child better handle transitions by visualizing everyday activities and getting important information about timing and duration.
Currently for iPad devices.

Time Timer (for ages 7 and up)

Time Timer LLC, www.timetimer.com
This easy-to-tailor timing app displays the minutes remaining in an activity as a red disk that becomes smaller as time elapses. Up to four timers can be set for different activities, and a tap of the disk

at any time reveals a numerical readout of the time remaining. **Price: $1.99 to $4.99.**

Benefit: This program can help a child who struggles with task completion to improve both focus and productivity.
Currently for iPad and Android devices.

SOCIAL LEARNING APPS

Calm Counter (for ages 5 and up)

Touch Autism, www.touchautism.com
This app teaches self awareness and the recognition of positive ways to manage anger and anxiety. A social story is included that explains how to calm down. There are also practice exercises to reinforce self-control. **Price: $2.99.**

Benefit: Calm Counter offers children practice using visual cues, counting backward, and breathing patterns to help control their emotions.
Currently for iPad and Android devices.

How Would You Feel If . . . (for ages 6 and up)

Super Duper Publications, www.superduperinc.com
This app includes fifty-six illustrated picture cards with audio that reads the question on each card, such as, "How would you feel if your favorite football team lost?" Illustrations depict a variety of life situations and are intended to lead to discussion of a child's reaction and feelings. Both appropriate and incorrect responses receive feedback, and a child's results can be viewed on a graph. **Price: $1.99.**

Benefit: This app can help children with special needs recognize and verbalize personal reactions to social situations. The activity teaches appropriate behavior and also builds communication skills.
Currently for iPad devices.

Model Me Going Places (for ages 3 and up)

Model Me Kids, www.modelmekids.com
This app presents slide shows of children modeling appropriate behavior in everyday places such as school, a store, or a restaurant. Each slide is accompanied by audio narration and descriptive text. Be aware that the app contains advertisements for the company's line of social-skills DVDs. **Price: Free.**

Benefit: This app can help reinforce expected behavior and lessen the fear of new places in a child with autism or Asperger syndrome. Currently for iPad and Android devices.

My DPS (for ages 6 and up)

The Language Express, Inc., http://thesocialexpress.com
This digital problem solver (DPS) shows videos of social situations to help a child identify feelings and coping strategies. Eight feelings and four coping strategies are available to choose from, and a child's own pictures and text can be added to personalize the app. **Price: $.99.**

Benefit: My DPS can help children with autism spectrum disorders or developmental delays to improve their social proficiency and manage their emotions.
Currently for iPad and Android devices.

Social Adventures (for ages 5 and up)

all4mychild, www.all4mychild.com
This parent-created app offers an eight-week social skills awareness program that can double as individual lessons as needed for practicing relationship behaviors and initiating interactions. **Price: $19.99.**

Benefit: Designed for children with autism spectrum disorders and social difficulties, this app offers practice in thinking about and behaving in the expected manner during social situations.
Currently for iPad devices.

Touch and Learn—Emotions (for ages 4 and up)

Innovative Mobile Apps, Ltd, www.appolearning.com
This app uses photos of children with different facial expressions to provide safe practice in recognizing feelings. Accompanying audio guides the user in trying to identify which child is showing which emotion. **Price: Free.**

Benefit: This program can help children with developmental delays learn to read body language and recognize and name common emotions.
Currently for iPad devices.

SPEECH AND COMMUNICATION APPS

Gabby Tabs—AAC for Kids (for all ages)

Tech Unlimited, www.gabbytabs.com
This easy-to-use app provides three customizable categories, or tabs, of things to talk about. Within each tab are six buttons that play a customized audible message when tapped. Three key words are also available within each category. **Price: $9.99.**

Benefit: Gabby Tabs can serve as a child-friendly augmentative and alternative communication (AAC) device, enabling a nonverbal child to communicate at home, at school, and on the go.
Currently for iPad and Android devices.

iCommunicate (for all ages)

Grembe, Inc., www.grembe.com
This customizable multipurpose app allows users to create visual schedules, communication boards, choice boards, storyboards, and flashcards using provided or personal audio and pictures. Boards are interactive, with swipes used to move pictures back and forth and one or two fingers used to add checkmarks and "do not" symbols to help transitions. **Price: $49.99.**

Benefit: iCommunicate provides visual supports to help children on the autism spectrum and those with language or intellectual disabilities to understand and follow routines, recognize and learn the correct pronunciation of words, make their own stories, and convey their thoughts and wishes.
Currently for iPad devices.

iPractice Verbs (for ages 5 and up)

Smarty Ears, www.smarty-ears.com
This app has two modes: Flashcards, for practicing verbs alone or in phrases and sentences, and Find It, a multiple-choice game for matching images and verbs. Colorful, child-friendly images are used throughout, and audio reinforcement praises correct answers and responds to mistakes with encouragement to try again. **Price: $9.99.**

Benefit: This program can help children with language delays to focus attention while learning to use correct verb tenses and subject-verb agreement when speaking.
Currently for iPad and Android devices.

Proloquo2Go (for all ages)

AssistiveWare, www.assistiveware.com
This augmentative and alternative communication (AAC) app allows a child to generate speech by tapping symbols or typing on an onscreen keyboard. Selected words are spoken aloud to enable immediate communication. Over 14,000 symbols are included, and as an alternative, a personal photo library can be used. Grammar support, word prediction, and social media sharing are part of this app. **Price: $219.99.**

Benefit: This app allows preverbal and nonverbal children to speak in a natural-sounding voice simply by choosing and tapping symbols on the screen.
Currently for iPad devices.

Rainbow Sentences (for ages 5 and up)

Mobile Education Store LLC, www.mobile-educationstore.com
This program color-codes the *who, what, where,* and *why* parts of sentences as the user chooses from provided words to make a sentence about a picture. Words are spoken as they are dragged and dropped, and there are six difficulty levels. Rewards are earned along the way. **Price: $7.99.**

Benefit: This app can help a child with language delays to recognize parts of sentences and understand how to combine the parts to form grammatically correct sentences.
Currently for iPad devices.

Speech Therapy for Apraxia—Words (for all ages)

Blue Whale Apps, www.bluewhaleapps.com
Sometimes called *NACD Home Speech Therapist*, this app provides practice in pronouncing nineteen consonant sounds. Eight different practice levels allow a child to learn appropriate mouth and tongue movements for speech production. Illustrations and audio accompany each syllable, and articulation drills are also available. **Price: $4.99.**

Benefit: This app can help children with speech delays to learn and practice correct speech sound production and ultimately minimize articulation errors.
Currently for Android devices.

APPS FOR HEARING IMPAIRMENTS

AutismXpress (for ages 3 and up)

SQUISH, www.squishgames.com
This app, which was designed for use with children on the autism spectrum, includes three activities—Feeling, Finder, Emotion

Matching, and Expression Questions—that can develop a child's ability to understand goals, intentions, behaviors, and responses in the absence of auditory information. Included are animated illustrations, a matching activity, and a text-accompanied question/answer game for adult and child. **Price: $1.99.**

Benefit: AutismXpress can help hearing impaired youngsters and others recognize situations and identify and express their feelings, thereby building speech and communication skills as well as social awareness.

Currently for iPad and Android devices.

Baby Sign and Learn (for all ages)

Baby Sign and Learn, www.babysignandlearn.com
This American Sign Language app offers animated videos, flashcards, and an interactive quiz for adult and child to use together. **Price: $2.99.**

Benefit: This app can help children with all levels of hearing impairments, as it also supports the learning of spoken language through narrative that accompanies the teaching of signs. This app is highly recommended by speech therapists.

Currently for iPad and Android devices.

Danny the Dragon Meets Jimmy (for all ages)

iStorytime, www.istorytime.com
This award-winning children's book app follows the adventures of a lovable dragon and can be told with help from an animated sign language interpreter who pops up on the side of each page. **Price: $2.99.**

Benefit: This app combines vivid illustrations, text, and sign language to promote the art of friendship and the virtue of kindness to hearing-impaired children.

Currently for iPad devices.

HOPE Words (for ages 3 and up)

Cochlear LTD, http://hope.CochlearAmericas.com
This application features interactive alphabet flashcards that, when touched, enlarge along with a voice narration of the letter name and sound from a leading auditory verbal therapist. **Price: $1.99.**

Benefit: HOPE Words can help children with cochlear implants and other hearing impairments practice matching their speech production to what they hear.
Currently for iPad devices.

Old MacDonald HD (for all ages)

Duck Duck Moose, www.duckduckmoose.com
Developed by language specialists and early childhood teachers, this award-winning app contains creative activities and music that let the user engage with friendly characters and animals. Surprises are contained in each of twelve interactive pages. **Price: $.99.**

Benefit: This app can help children with hearing impairments and other youngsters improve their listening and language skills as well as their motor development.
Currently for iPad devices.

What's That Sound? (for ages 2 and up)

Different Roads to Learning, Inc., www.difflearn.com
In this app, children match objects with their respective sounds by first listening, then choosing from among several pictures to tap the source of the sound. **Price: $1.99.**

Benefit: This program can improve listening, sound recognition, and auditory processing skills as children work to identify and discriminate between everyday noises.
Currently for iPad devices. (Note that a very similar app for Android devices, "What's The Sound?" by NewMtoddlearn, can be purchased for $1.99 in the Google Play store.)

FINE MOTOR APPS

Bubbles (for ages 2 and up)

Hog Bay Software, https://itunes.apple.com/us/genre/ios/id36?mt=8
With this program, children create brilliantly colored bubbles on the screen with the tap of a finger. Another touch causes the bubbles to pop to entertaining sound effects. There is an in-app option to purchase other pictures such as balloons, leaves, or fireworks for $.99 each. **Price: $.99.**

Benefit: This app helps a child with fine motor delays to improve finger dexterity and eye-hand coordination. It also reinforces cause-and-effect relationships.
Currently for iPad devices. (Note that a highly similar Android app, also called Bubbles, by Squishy Things Inc., is available free of charge in the Google Play store.)

Dexteria (for ages 4 and up)

BinaryLabs, Inc., www.dexteria.net
Dexteria is a collection of therapeutic but fun hand exercises designed to improve finger sequencing and finger isolation. The user can choose from three options: Write It, Pinch It, and Tap It, each of which includes colorful screens and narrated activities. There are several difficulty levels, and helpful feedback is provided. **Price: $3.99.**

Benefit: Dexteria can help increase a child's fine motor speed, strength, and dexterity while improving the eye-hand control needed for writing.
Currently for iPad devices.

Dot to Dot Numbers and Letters (for ages 4 and up)

Apps in My Pocket, Ltd., www.appsinmypocket.com
This program includes animation, graphics, and sounds in forty-two dot-to-dot puzzles. As the correct dot is touched in sequence,

the name of the next dot is announced. When a puzzle is completed, a picture appears. A leaderboard displays the best scores, and age-based settings are available. **Price: $1.99.**

Benefit: This app allows the practice of number and letter recognition, counting, and the alphabet while helping a child improve eye-hand and fine motor control.

Currently for iPad devices. (Note that a very similar Android app, Dot to Dot Letters and Numbers by puzzle.tv, is available for $.99 in the Google Play store.)

Drawing Pad (for ages 5 and up)

Darren Murtha Design, Inc., www.murthadesign.com
Drawing Pad allows users to create beautiful art with crayons, pencils, markers, paintbrushes, and more. The child selects a background and taps a desired device from a side toolbar. Picture stickers can be added, and finished work can be shared on social media. **Price: $1.99.**

Benefit: This app helps a child with weaker finger dexterity improve eye-hand and fine motor skills. Stylus users have ready access to the items on the toolbar.

Currently for Android devices.

Uncolor Dogs (for ages 2 and up)

ChristyBrantCo, LLC, www.appsmenow.com/seller/364904380-ChristyBrantCo_LLC
In this program, an image is slowly revealed by erasing a solid-colored screen with fingers, the thumb, or the whole hand. Uncovered pictures contain surprises, such as a dog sitting in a bubble bath. **Price: $.99.**

Benefit: Uncolor Dogs can help children with developmental delays improve eye-hand control while learning about cause-and-effect relationships.

Currently for iPad devices.

Wheels on the Bus (for ages 3 and up)

Duck Duck Moose, Inc., www.duckduckmoose.com
This app allows users to spin, slide, tap, and sweep objects on animated illustrations according to narrated instructions and the classic children's song. Different musical instruments are identified as they play in the background, and a child's own voice can be added. **Price: $1.99.**

Benefit: This program can encourage eye-hand coordination, language, and thinking skills in children with fine motor or developmental delays.
Currently for iPad and Android devices.

APPS FOR VISUAL IMPAIRMENTS

Balloonimals (for all ages)

IDEO, www.ideotoylab.com
This app uses high-contrast colors on a white background. Children touch the screen to blow up, play with, and pop various balloon animals. **Price: $2.99.**

Benefit: Balloonimals teaches cause-and-effect relationships while improving a child's focus and eye-hand skills.
Currently for iPad and Android devices.

EDA Play (for ages 2 and up)

EDA Play, www.edaplay.com
EDA Play includes two four-level apps, Visual and Task, allowing for customization to individual needs. A child's voice directs the user to perform tasks of increasing difficulty, from touching particular images to completing or connecting shapes. Progress is recorded. **Price: $4.99.**

Benefit: This app helps children improve their visual processing and fine motor skills.
Currently for iPad devices.

Knee Bouncers Big Little Games, Volumes 1 through 4 (for ages 1 and up)

Kneebouncers, www.kneebouncers.com
The activities in this four-volume series of apps use simple, brightly colored, touchable graphics and familiar sounds that respond to every touch or swipe. Each version has four to five easy games that encourage screen interaction. **Price: $1.99.**

Benefit: This app provides fine motor practice and visual tracking exercise while teaching a child about cause and effect.
Currently for Android devices.

My Talking Picture Board (for all ages)

Little Bear Sees and the Western Pennsylvania School for Blind Children, www.littlebearsees.org
In this app, boards are set up with pictures from an iPad photo library that can be sized, grouped, and placed on different backgrounds according to the desired level of difficulty. The child interacts with a preset Play screen, earning onscreen rewards for touching requested objects. **Price: $19.99.**

Benefit: This program helps children with cortical visual impairment and other vision problems learn to locate and recognize two-dimensional images.
Currently for iPad devices.

Peekaboo Barn (for ages 2 and up)

Night and Day Studios, https://itunes.apple.com/us/genre/ios/id36?mt=8 *or* https://play.google.com/store/apps?hl=en
This app uses a barn setting and simple pictures and sounds to encourage children to guess which animals are hiding behind various doors. **Price: $1.99.**

Benefit: This program can help children with visual impairment to practice eye-hand skills, understand cause and effect, and learn familiar sounds and animal names.
Currently for iPad and Android devices.

Sensory Light Box (for ages 3 and up)

Cognable, www.cognable.com

This app features a black screen on which twenty-one visual and auditory options such as "Rain" or "Explode" await the user's touch. When an option is selected, different sound and light creations happen at the touch of a finger and continue until the finger is removed. **Price: $2.99.**

Benefit: Children with visual impairment or intellectual disability can use this app for fine motor exercise, practice tracking images, and understanding cause-and-effect relationships.
Currently for iPad and Android devices.

READING APPS

abc PocketPhonics (for ages 3 and up)

Apps in My Pocket, Ltd., www.appsinmypocket.com
This app uses animation and audio to teach letters, sounds, and first words. Children trace letters as they hear their sounds, select letters to match sounds, and listen to the pronunciation and spelling of early reading words. **Price: $2.99.**

Benefit: This app can help a child learn small groups of letter sounds and blend those sounds to form words. Letter-writing practice is included to spur improvement in eye-hand and fine motor skills.
Currently for iPad devices.

Action Sight Words Games (for ages 4 and up)

22Learn, www.22learn.com
This program features more than 300 sight words—words such as "the"—which lack letter-sound correspondence and have to be mem-

orized. Six action-packed, easy-to-play activities involve listening to, recognizing, matching, spelling, and reading sight words. **Price: $1.99.**

Benefit: This app provides a child with valuable practice in the recognition of sight words, an important part of becoming a fluent reader.

Currently for Android and iPad devices.

Bluster! (for ages 6 and up)

McGraw Hill School Education Group, www.mheonline.com
This app offers practice in recognizing root words, homophones (sound-alike words), rhymes, and other word-structure similarities. The activity has five levels of difficulty and can be played in individual or team modes. Users swipe through a word list to find three related words—"unfit," "undo," and "unlike," for instance—and drag the matching words to an onscreen scoring area. Be aware that although the app is free, expansion activities such as "Extra Prefixes" cost $.99 each. **Price: Free.**

Benefit: Bluster! can boost a child's reading, vocabulary, and phonics skills through word analysis work involving rhyming, prefixes and suffixes, and more.

Currently for iPad devices.

First Words With Phonics (for ages 3 and up)

Anlock, www.anlock.com
This app allows users to choose from pictures of thirty different animals and explore their colorful habitats while hearing associated sounds and viewing letters of the alphabet as they float onto the screen. The letters, which are accompanied by audio that identifies their names and phonetic sounds, eventually combine to spell the animals' names. Letter and color hints are given if needed, and the app has six different difficulty levels. **Price: $2.49.**

Benefit: This program provides all children—especially those with speech, hearing, or attention difficulties—with an interactive way to recognize letter names and sounds, and to learn how letters can combine to create words.

Currently for iPad and Windows 8.1 devices.

SUPER WHY! (for ages 4 and up)

PBS Kids, www.pbskids.org

This app, based on the PBS Kids television show of the same name, contains four games to help build reading skills. Stickers are awarded for successfully completing each game, and helpful characters teach children that it's okay to make mistakes. **Price: $2.99.**

Benefit: SUPER WHY! encourages sustained attention and offers an engaging way for struggling readers to practice letter sounds, rhyming, spelling, and writing.

Currently for iPad and Android devices.

Word Magic (for ages 3 and up)

Anusen Inc., www.anusen.com

In this application, a picture is shown with one or more letters missing from its name. The child uses knowledge of letter sounds to choose letters that complete the word. The ability level can be set so that blanks appear at the front, middle, or end of the word, and words of three to six letters can be preset. The sound of children's cheering voices is heard whenever a word is spelled correctly, and stars appear as a reward after five successive correct answers are given. **Price: $.99.**

Benefit: This program can strengthen a struggling reader's understanding of the relationship between letters, sounds, and words while also improving sight word vocabulary and spelling skills.

Currently for iPad and Android devices.

WRITING APPS

iWriteWords (for ages 5 and up)

gigglelab, www.giggle-lab.com

This app encourages letter writing practice. Children drag a red crab over a series of numbered balls that are placed in a letter shape. When all the letters in a word are drawn, a cute picture appears and the word slides into a hole. Accompanying audio names the letters and spells the words aloud. **Price: $2.99.**

Benefit: iWriteWords can help a child develop the eye-hand and fine motor control necessary for writing while also improving letter and word recognition skills.

Currently for iPad devices.

LetterSchool (for ages 4 and up)

Sanoma Media Netherlands B.V., www.letterschool.com

This award-winning app uses a three-stage approach—tap, trace, and write—to teach letter and number writing, counting, and letter sounds. Flowers, candy, trains, animals, and other brilliant graphics are used in conjunction with sound effects and animations to engage the user as she learns to recognize and write the alphabet and numbers from 1 to 10. **Price: $2.99.**

Benefit: LetterSchool targets a child's fine motor skills and eye-hand coordination as it teaches letter formation, sounds, and names, as well as the writing and reading of numbers.

Currently for iPad and Android devices.

Sentence Builder (for ages 6 and up)

Mobile Education Store, www.mobile-educationstore.com

This program provides a simple and fun environment in which to practice the building of grammatically correct sentences. The easy-to-use app includes three levels of play, encouragement animations, audio clips, and one hundred pictures around which to build sentences. **Price: $5.99.**

Benefit: Sentence Builder can help a child with communication or writing delays to hear, read, recognize, and use correct sentence structure.
Currently for iPad devices.

Share My ABCs (for ages 3 and up)

Offficial, https://itunes.apple.com/us/genre/ios/id36?mt=8
This program uses a bright landscape and two modes—practice and guided—to help children learn to trace the alphabet, words, and animals. Words and phrases can also be created, and the results can be viewed in a gallery and shared via social media. Progress can be tracked, and the level of difficulty can be changed. **Price: $4.99.**

Benefit: Share My ABCs can help children with fine motor and visual tracking delays to improve these skills as they learn to recognize and write the letters of the alphabet.
Currently for iPad devices.

Storybook Maker (for ages 4 and up)

Merge Mobile, www.mergemobile.com
This easy-to-use book-making app guides children through the writing and publishing of their own original stories. Each book page can be customized using text, different background and border styles, stickers, personal photos, paintings, and recorded audio. Finished works can be shared with others through various social media. **Price: $3.99.**

Benefit: This program can encourage creativity and provide practice with sentence structure and storytelling in children who struggle with writing.
Currently for iPad devices.

Wet-Dry-Try Suite for Capitals, Numbers & Lowercase (for ages 4 and up)

Handwriting Without Tears, www.wetdrytry.com
This interactive chalkboard app groups letters and numbers by shape for easier mastery and includes a coach who helps with friendly audio cues. There are three levels of difficulty, two options for screen sensitivity, and a star reward system when a level is mastered. **Price: $6.99.**

Benefit: This app uses a multisensory approach that can help children with fine motor and eye-hand delays learn to write using correct letter and number formations.
Currently for iPad devices.

APPS FOR MATH

BugMath (for ages 3 and up)

TotsMobile, www.totsmobile.com
In this app, children help an alien whose spaceship has crashed on a planet of bugs. Stickers are collected for his spaceship as a child counts, matches, orders, adds, and subtracts groups of bugs in arcade-like games. **Price: $1.95.**

Benefit: BugMath offers a way to help children with math or developmental delays understand, practice, and remember basic mathematics skills.
Currently for iPad and Android devices.

DragonBox Algebra 5+ (for ages 5 and up)

We Want to Know, www.dragonboxapp.com
This app teaches the very basics of algebra in a gradual way, with users moving at their own pace as they follow instructions to solve puzzles in a playful, colorful game environment. Two hundred puz-

zles cover addition, multiplication, and division, along with the fundamentals of simple equations. *DragonBox Algebra 12+* is available for older children. **Price: $5.99.**

Benefit: This app can help children who struggle with math concepts to master basic algebraic operations in a fun, stress-free way. Currently for iPad, Android, and Windows 8.1 devices.

Elmo Loves 123s (for ages 3 and up)

Sesame Workshop, www.sesameworkshop.org
This award-winning application uses simple games, classic *Sesame Street* video clips, color-by-number pictures, jigsaw puzzles, and other activities to present and reinforce the numbers 1 through 20. The app enables adults to easily track their child's work and play. **Price: $4.99.**

Benefit: Elmo helps young children—as well as older youngsters who struggle with basic math concepts—to learn math readiness skills such as number recognition, number writing, counting, adding, and subtracting.
Currently for iPad and Android devices.

Marble Math Junior and *Marble Math* (for ages 5–8 and 9–12)

Artgig Studio, www.artgigapps.com
These applications allow children to solve various math problems with numbers collected as marbles are rolled through a series of mazes. Audio is present for emerging readers, and there are three separate difficulty levels to choose from. If desired, game play can be customized to concentrate on specific math concepts. **Price: $2.99 each.**

Benefit: Both *Marble Math* apps provide practice with important math concepts while also benefitting a child's fine motor skills and eye-hand coordination.
Currently for iPad devices.

Scout's 123 Carnival (for ages 2 and up)

LeapFrog Enterprises, Inc., www.leapfrog.com
This program uses animation, games, and an interactive carnival scene to teach the numbers 1 through 20. Characters Scout and Violet can be preset to say a child's name, birthday, and favorite things during the activities. A Parent Zone allows adults to track children's progress, and five awards are given as a child learns to identify and count groups of numbers. **Price: $1.99.**

Benefit: The personalized aspect of this program helps engage a child as she improves number recognition, counting skills, and eye-hand coordination.
Currently for iPad devices.

YodelOh Math Mountain (for ages 5 and up)

Spinlight Studio, www.spinlight.com
In this mountain-climbing app, the user performs simple math computations and taps the correct answer on the screen to keep Hans from being chased by sheep or falling off a cliff. **Price: $2.99.**

Benefit: This fast-paced app can help a child learn addition, subtraction, and multiplication facts while also improving focus and visual tracking skills.
Currently for iPad and Android devices.

Conclusion

E very consumer knows that technology is ever-changing, so it doesn't make sense to aim for the newest tablet, the most cutting-edge add-on, or the just-released app. After all, another device or program will surely claim that title within a matter of days. Instead, you need to focus on acquiring the tablet that best suits your budget and your child, the add-ons that make the tablet most accessible to your youngster, and the apps that are most likely to inspire growth in skill areas that need improvement. Always keep an eye on both the changing needs of your child and the evolving world of technology so that, over time, you can continue to offer your youngster the most appropriate educational tools available.

I hope this book has provided the guidance you need to navigate the world of tablets and educational apps. As you work with your young learner, I'd love to hear about your experiences as well as any suggestions you may have for future editions of this book. Please feel free to email me at breakingthrough.tablets.apps@ gmail.com. Or, if you prefer, you can write me care of Square One Publishers, 115 Herricks Road, Garden City Park, NY 11040.

I wish you and your child the best of luck.

Glossary

On occasion, terminology is used in this book that is common to the world of technology or the field of special education but may not be completely familiar to you. To help in this regard, definitions are provided below for a number of terms. If you find that you need explanations of computer-related words that have not been included here, turn to page 124 of the Resources list, which will guide you to extensive online technological glossaries. All words that appear below in *italic type* are defined within the glossary.

adaptive equipment. Any device or piece of *software* that assists people with disabilities. In computers, examples include specially designed *keyboards* and mice, alternative communication programs, and special *styluses* that are easy to grasp and use.

Android. The *operating system*, or *platform*, that was developed by Android, Inc. (and eventually purchased by Google) primarily for use in mobile devices such as *tablets* and smartphones.

anxiety disorder. An umbrella term for a number of different disorders that are characterized by pervasive apprehension, worrying, or uncertainty about real or imagined events. This excessive anxiety can lead to physical and psychological health problems. Types of anxiety disorders include *generalized anxiety disorder, obsessive-compulsive disorder, phobia, post-traumatic stress disorder, separation anxiety disorder,* and *social anxiety disorder.*

app (application). A small, specialized program that can be run on *tablets,* smartphones, and other mobile devices.

apraxia. A neurological condition, either acquired or developed, in which people find it hard or impossible to perform certain motor movements even though they have normal muscles. One type, apraxia of speech, refers to difficulty in planning and coordinating the muscle movements needed to produce spoken words.

Asperger syndrome. This *autism spectrum disorder,* also known as Asperger disorder or Asperger's, is characterized by restricted interests, repetitive behavior patterns, and great difficulty with social interaction. Despite often having above-average intelligence, people with this syndrome tend to demonstrate limited empathy and an inability to understand the facial expressions and body language of others.

attention deficit hyperactivity disorder (ADHD). A chronic condition characterized by a number of developmentally inappropriate behaviors, including hyperactivity, impulsivity, and difficulty sustaining attention. In children, conditions secondary to ADHD can include low self-esteem, social difficulties, and poor school performance.

auditory processing disorder. An umbrella term covering a number of conditions that affect the way the brain processes language and sounds. While people with this disorder—which is sometimes called central auditory processing disorder, or CAPD—have normal ear structure and function, a dysfunction in the brain causes them to struggle to recognize and interpret sounds and speech.

augmentative and alternative communication (AAC). A form of communication other than oral language that is used to express needs, wants, and ideas. While the term includes gestures and facial expressions, AAC most often refers to *tablets* and other electronic devices that enable or enhance the communication of people who have difficulty speaking.

autism spectrum disorder (ASD). Also called autism, this term refers to a group of complex disorders of brain development that are characterized by varying levels of difficulty with verbal and nonverbal communication, social interaction, and repetitive behaviors. ASDs include *Pervasive Developmental Disorder Not Otherwise Specified (PDD-NOS), Asperger syndrome,* and *autistic disorder.*

autistic disorder. The most severe form of *autism spectrum disorder,* characterized by problems with focus, communication, and socialization. Repetitive behaviors are common, as are academic difficulties.

Bluetooth technology. A globally available technology that allows billions of mobile devices to connect to and communicate with one another over a short range without the need for wires or cables. The most common Bluetooth-enabled devices are smartphones, *tablets,* medical equipment, and home entertainment machines.

cellular network. A communications network, also called a mobile network, that consists of land areas, or cells, that use differing sets of radio frequencies to allow mobile devices to connect wirelessly and without interference. Each cellular network is served by at least one fixed-location transceiver, or base station.

central auditory processing disorder. See *auditory processing disorder.*

central hearing impairment. A type of hearing loss that is caused not by damage to the ear, but by damage to or impairment of the nerves or cells of the central nervous system, either in the pathways to the brain or in the brain itself. This impairs the individual's ability to recognize and interpret sounds and language.

central processing unit. See *processor.*

cochlear implant. A small electronic device that can provide a sense of sound to someone who is profoundly deaf or severely hearing impaired. It consists of an external device worn behind the ear and a second portion that is surgically implanted beneath the skin.

concussion. See *traumatic brain injury.*

conductive hearing impairment. A type of hearing loss caused by disease or obstruction in the outer or middle ear, making sound difficult to perceive.

connectivity. The ability of a computer program or device to link with other programs and devices.

cortical visual impairment (CVI). A disorder in which the eyes and optic nerves appear healthy, but vision is impaired due to one of a number of conditions affecting the cortex, or surface, of the brain.

degenerative disease. A type of disease in which the function or structure of the affected body tissues or organs increasingly deteriorates over time. Osteoarthritis and muscular dystrophy are two examples.

desktop computer. A personal computer intended for use at a single location and not suitable for mobile use.

dysregulation. Impairment of one of the body's regulatory mechanisms that control metabolism, organ function, or immune response. Dysregulation of the brain, for instance, can result from *traumatic brain injury (TBI).*

eye-hand coordination. Sometimes referred to as visual motor skill or hand-eye coordination, this is the ability to use information taken in by the eyes to control and direct the hands as they execute a given task.

fine motor skills. Skills involving small movements of the hands, wrists, fingers, feet, toes, lips, and tongue that enable the individual to complete small tasks such as grasping an object with the thumb and forefinger.

finger dexterity. The strength, flexibility, and controlled movements of the fingers while manipulating small objects such as *keyboard* keys or a pencil.

free app. Sometimes called a lite app, this program can be downloaded without charge as an introduction to the full version of the application.

generalized anxiety disorder. An umbrella term describing a condition of chronic anxiety, exaggerated worry, and stress even when there is little or no cause for concern.

gigabytes (GB). A measure of computer data storage capacity equal to one billion bytes.

gigahertz (GHz). A measure of frequency, equal to one billion hertz, that is an indicator of a computer's processing speed.

graphics. The set of technologies used to produce, display, and manipulate pictorial images on a computer screen. This term also refers to the images themselves.

hand-eye coordination. See *eye-hand coordination.*

hardware. The physical parts of a computer system, such as the motherboard and hard drive.

hearing impairment. A loss in hearing that prevents an individual from normally receiving sounds. Categories of hearing impairment include *central hearing impairment, conductive hearing impairment, mixed hearing impairment,* and *sensorineural hearing impairment.*

icon. An onscreen pictogram, or symbol, that helps the computer user navigate the computer system or a particular program.

intellectual disability (ID). Once called mental retardation, a generalized disorder resulting in significant impairment in cognitive ability and the acquisition of life skills.

interface. The point of interaction or contact between the computer user and the device or its *software.* When using a tablet, the interface is provided by the *touchscreen.*

iOS. The mobile *operating system,* or *platform,* developed and distributed by Apple, Inc., for its iPhone, iPod Touch, and iPad.

keyboard. In computers, the primary device used to input text. The arrangement of the keyboard is modeled after that of a typewriter, but also contains additional keys to control function. A computer keyboard can be physical (traditional) or virtual. In the latter case, the keyboard is projected onto a *touchscreen.*

laptop. A personal computer that is small enough to be easily carried by hand and used on your lap, but has the basic capabilities of a *desktop computer.*

learning disability. A condition that makes it difficult for the brain to process, understand, and use information, and therefore affects a child's ability to learn in a specific subject area such as reading or math.

lite app. See *free app.*

low vision. The bilateral (affecting both sides) partial loss of eyesight that cannot be corrected with regular eyeglasses or contact lenses, and can make everyday tasks difficult or impossible to accomplish.

mixed hearing impairment. A type of *hearing impairment* that involves problems in both the outer or middle ear and the inner ear, making it a combination of *conductive hearing impairment* and *sensorineural hearing impairment.*

mobile network. See *cellular network.*

musculoskeletal disorder. One of a variety of conditions affecting the muscles, bones, and joints, and therefore causing pain and/or weakness that can interfere with everyday activities. Rheumatoid arthritis is an example.

netbook. A portable computer that is smaller, lighter in weight, and less expensive than a *laptop.* Unlike a *tablet,* a netbook includes a traditional *keyboard,* which can make it easier to type lengthy documents.

neuromotor impairment. A problem with the brain, spinal cord, or nervous system that is acquired at or prior to birth and can result in complex motor issues. Examples include spina bifida and cerebral palsy.

neuroplasticity. The brain's ability to reorganize and restore itself after injury or illness by forming new neural connections to replace those that were damaged or severed.

obsessive-compulsive disorder (OCD). A disorder that involves the controlling of pervasive apprehension or worry through repetitive actions aimed at reducing anxiety, such as counting rituals or excessive hand-washing.

operating system. The collection of *software* that runs a computer's basic functions. *Windows* and *iOS* are well-known examples.

orthopedic impairment (OI). An impairment of the body's musculoskeletal system that severely impacts a child's educational performance. OIs are generally categorized as *degenerative diseases, musculoskeletal disorders,* or *neuromotor impairments.*

Pervasive Developmental Disorder Not Otherwise Specified (PDD-NOS). A condition that is characterized by social and communication difficulties, but does not have sufficient symptoms or intensity to be called autism. Nevertheless, the problems caused by PDD-NOS affect a child's social abilities and academic growth.

phobia. A persistent, irrational fear of and desire to avoid a specific object, activity, or situation.

platform. The underlying computer system (*software*) on which software applications run. Generally, a computer's platform is its *operating system,* such as *Windows* or *iOS.*

post-traumatic stress disorder (PTSD). An *anxiety disorder* that develops after exposure to extreme emotional trauma.

processor. Also called a central processing unit (CPU), this internal computer hardware carries out the instructions of a computer program.

random access memory (RAM). A computer's data storage that allows information to be accessed quickly from random locations on a memory module. RAM is measured in *gigabytes.*

sensorineural hearing impairment. A type of *hearing impairment* that results from damage to the cochlea—the organ of balance and hearing found in the inner ear—and/or the auditory nerve that supplies it. The result is difficulty in hearing certain frequencies and, in turn, a distortion in hearing.

separation anxiety disorder. A form of *anxiety disorder* characterized by a child's significant fear and nervousness when separated from a parent or caregiver. The fear of separation can cause physical symptoms and interfere with everyday activities such as playing with friends or going to school.

short-term memory. A limited-capacity memory that allows an individual to keep small bits of information in mind for a brief period of time. For instance, short-term memory can enable you to remember a phone number long enough to write it down on a piece of paper.

social anxiety disorder. A type of *anxiety disorder* characterized by a child's excessive fear of social situations in which he might be watched and judged by other people.

social media. Virtual communities through which people share information and ideas. Facebook, Twitter, and LinkedIn are three popular examples.

software. Organized collections of computer data and instructions that are generally divided into two categories. System software provides the basic functions of a computer; in other words, it runs the computer. Application software is used to perform specific tasks, such as word processing.

specifications (specs). The specific details of components built into a device, such as the memory, connectivity, and storage capacity of a *tablet*.

speech recognition software. See *speech-to-text software*.

speech/language impairment. A variety of conditions that interfere with communication and show themselves as errors in sound or word production, fluency, or vocal quality.

speech-to-text software. Computer *software* designed to recognize spoken words and display them as onscreen text. This is also referred to as speech recognition software.

stylus. A thin, sometimes pointed pen-shaped instrument that is used to write, draw, or tap key locations on a tablet or other mobile device.

tablet. A single-panel mobile computer chiefly distinguished by its use of a *touchscreen*—rather than a *keyboard* and mouse—as an input device.

text-to-speech software. Computer *software* designed to convert text and documents to speech, allowing words to be read aloud to the computer user.

3G and 4G technology. The third generation (3G) and fourth generation (4G) of mobile, or cellular, technology. As the names suggest, 3G and 4G follow two earlier generations, with each new generation representing an upgrade in the speed of information transfer to a mobile device.

touchpad. A touch-sensitive surface of a *laptop* or *netbook* computer that allows a user to control the cursor, or pointer, that appears on the device's display screen.

touchscreen. A touch-sensitive display screen that enables a computer user to control a program through simple gestures such as tapping or sliding the fingers.

traumatic brain injury (TBI). Often called a concussion, an injury that occurs when an external force or blow causes the brain to move within the skull, stretching and tearing delicate nerve fibers.

USB port. A connection, formally called a Universal Serial Bus port, that allows users to attach stand-alone devices such as *keyboards* and mice to a computer via cables.

visual impairment. Any type of vision loss, whether total or partial. The two main categories of visual impairment are *cortical visual impairment* and *low vision.*

visual motor skills. See *eye-hand coordination.*

visual processing. Sometimes called visual perception, the ability to interpret the environment and solve problems by understanding and using information taken in by the eyes.

Wi-Fi networking. A technology, formally called Wireless Fidelity, that allows electronic devices such as *tablets* and smartphones to connect to the Internet or exchange information wirelessly within a particular area.

Windows. A personal computer *operating system* that has had many versions and includes standard business applications such as Microsoft Office and Excel.

word-prediction software. Computer *software* that reduces the number of keystrokes or screen taps necessary to type a word by anticipating the correct word after only a few characters. This is helpful not only in communication but also as a spelling aid.

Resources

Throughout this book, you have read about the electronic devices and software programs that can help your child develop important skills, better communicate with others, and enjoy a richer life. You have also discovered that there are websites and organizations that can help you as your family begins learning about and using tablet technology. The listings on the next few pages will enable you to easily obtain any further information you need. They begin with online glossaries that can assist you in understanding and comparing computer tablets so that you can make the best choice possible. After that, you'll find websites that present tablet reviews, app stores, and app reviews and recommendations. Finally, there's an extensive list of organizations that offer financial help and other forms of support to families with special needs youngsters. Note that the websites through which you can buy the specific apps recommended in this book are provided for each product in the list found on pages 90 to 110. What you'll find on pages 126 and 127 are general e-retailers that offer sizeable collections of many types of apps. The websites on which you can purchase the specific tablet add-ons and accessories recommended in this book are found in the list on pages 71 to 77.

GLOSSARIES OF TECHNOLOGICAL TERMS

NBT's Tablet Glossary

Website: www.pocketables.com/2012/03/nbts-tablet-glossary.html
This somewhat technical glossary of terms was compiled specifically to help visitors to the site understand posts. But the listing of terms and definitions can also be quite helpful when researching tablet features.

Smartphone and Tablet Glossary

Website: www.squidoo.com/smartphone-tablet-glossary
This glossary of commonly used technological terms—specifically, terms associated with tablets and smartphones—can be extremely valuable to tablet shoppers who wish to compare the features of various machines.

Tablet PC Glossary

Website: www.tabletpcexpert.co.uk/glossary/
This relatively short but helpful A-to-Z listing offers a variety of terms and definitions that are common to the world of tablet computing.

WEBSITES OFFERING TABLET REVIEWS AND COMPARISONS

c/net

Website: www.cnet.com
This technology news website provides reviews of numerous products and presents information, recommendations, and a buyer's guide for tablet shoppers.

Consumer Search

Website: www.consumersearch.com
This consumers' website features descriptions and recommendations in hundreds of product categories and includes links to a buying guide and reviews for tablet computers.

Tablet PC Comparison

Website: www.tabletpccomparison.net
This website uses a chart format to list the components of dozens of tablet computers. Browsers can compare devices by type, brand, or features, as desired.

MAGAZINE WEBSITES FEATURING TECHNOLOGY PRODUCT REVIEWS

Laptop

Website: www.laptopmag.com
This website provides detailed product reviews and buying tips for purchasers of laptops, tablets, smartphones, and apps.

PC

Website: www.pcmag.com
PC Magazine's website presents news, information, and product reviews. Included are links to the "Best Android Tablets," the "Best iPad Apps," "Tablet Buying Basics," etc.

PC World

Website: www.pcworld.com
The PC World website offers extensive information and articles related to personal computing, along with frequent product reviews and recommendations.

ONLINE APP STORES

Amazon Appstore

Website: www.amazon.com
Once you're on the Amazon website, use the "Search" box to find "apps." This easy-to-use store offers Amazon's Kindle tablets and a range of Android apps that have met strict quality control standards. The store offers a "Free App of the Day" feature as well as a "Test Drive" button that lets you try apps before buying.

Apps for Special Needs

Website: www.blog.momswithapps.com/apps-for-special-needs/
This site features special education apps developed by Moms With Apps to assist children and families. A detailed description, app screen shots, customer ratings, and a helpful "Customers Also Bought" section appear on each app's page.

Google Play Store

Website: https://play.google.com/store/apps?hl=en
Google's extensive collection of Android apps is separated into categories, including "Top Paid in Education" and "Top Free in Education," and also has an "Editor's Choice" feature.

iPad Apps Store

Website: https://itunes.apple.com/us/genre/ios/id36?mt=8
iTunes, Apple's own online store, offers close to 400,000 apps for its iPad line. An "Education" link takes you to a vast collection of learning apps with a page-top alphabet to streamline your search. The app store also has a special education section. The iPad line of tablets comes preloaded with an iTunes app through which you can browse and shop.

Windows Apps

Website: windows.microsoft.com/en-us/windows-8/apps#Cat=t1
Microsoft's Apps for Windows store, available for tablets with Windows 8.1 or Windows RT 8.1 operating systems, offers more than 500 education applications. A description, list of features, age recommendations, and numerous screen shots are available for each applications, along with star ratings and links to related apps. If your tablet has an older operating system, the website provides a link to further information about Windows 8.1.

WEBSITES OFFERING REVIEWS AND RECOMMENDATIONS OF GENERAL EDUCATIONAL APPS

Apps 4 Kids

Website: www.apps4kids.net
Devoted to sharing reviews of the best apps for kids, this site separates its recommendations by age, device, language, educational area, and games. There is also a "Free Apps" link and another link to the Smart Apps for Kids website, which reviews hundreds of free apps for preschoolers.

Best Apps for Kids

Website: www.bestappsforkids.com
Started by a mother of three who has broad knowledge of educational apps, this website offers extensive app reviews for the iPhone, iPod, iPad, and Nook. App descriptions are separated by age/grade, device, star rating, and educational category. There is also a "What's New" link as well as links to free apps, app giveaways, and promotional codes.

Best Kids Apps

Website: www.bestkidsapps.com
This website offers reviews of iPhone, iPad, and Android apps, separated by age and device type. Links are provided to bestsellers, educational apps, and free apps.

Commonsense Media

Website: www.commonsensemedia.org
Commonsense Media is dedicated to improving the lives of kids and families by providing trustworthy information and education about the world of media and technology. Its website offers reviews of apps, complete with age recommendations and ratings, as well as a "Best Apps & Games" link. Included is a guide to featured apps for children with learning differences, with apps separated by category and experience level.

Kids App Reviews

Website: www.kids-app-reviews.com
This website presents "apps for kids, approved by kids." Along with detailed descriptions of featured apps, you'll find promotional codes and a link to the free apps of the week.

WEBSITES OFFERING RECOMMENDATIONS AND REVIEWS OF SPECIAL NEEDS APPS

Apps for Children With Special Needs

Website: www.a4cwsn.com
This website offers app recommendations and reviews, along with app videos, "Editors' Choice" selections, and a link to free educational apps.

Bridging Apps

Website: www.bridgingapps.org
Using Insignio, a custom-built app tool, this site supports the parents, teachers, and therapists of children with special needs in finding appropriate apps for mobile devices. The website offers new app reviews, app selection expertise, and general support in the form of an online community.

Friendship Circle

Website: www.friendshipcircle.org/apps
The website of the Friendship Circle of Michigan—a nonprofit organization—presents app reviews to assist parents and teachers of children with learning challenges in finding the perfect special needs application.

iAutism

Website: www.iautism.info
This website presents reviews of iPad and Android apps that support children with autism and special needs. In addition to app lists, the site also offers monthly analyses of apps for autism, learning, and leisure.

Inov8 Educational Consulting

Website: www.inov8-ed.com
The inov8 Educational Consulting company works with educators and families of children with special needs to integrate effective assistive technology tools into their lives. Its website offers descriptions of apps designed for students with learning disabilities, reading disabilities, autism spectrum disorders, and developmental delays. It also offers a multi-part seminar series highlighting apps for particular educational needs.

ORGANIZATIONS AND FOUNDATIONS OFFERING GRANTS AND SUPPORT TO FAMILIES WITH SPECIAL NEEDS CHILDREN

ACT Today!

6330 Variel Avenue, Suite 102
Woodland Hills, CA 91367
Phone: 818-340-4010
Website: www.act-today.org
A national nonprofit organization, ACT Today! seeks to help families provide treatment, services, and support for children with autism spectrum disorder, enabling them to achieve their full potential. The group also strives to raise awareness of autism.

Apps for Children With Special Needs

Website: www.a4cwsn.com/ipad2-4u
The Apps For Children With Special Needs organization has an "iPads 4U" program created to gift as many children as possible with iPad technology. The group's website provides app recommendations, as well.

Association of Blind Citizens

PO Box 246
Holbrook, MA 02343
Phone: 781-961-1023
Website: www.blindcitizens.org
The Association of Blind Citizen's Assistive Technology Fund will provide funds to cover 50 percent of the retail price of adaptive devices or software for use by those with significant visual impairment who meet eligibility requirements.

Autism Speaks Family Services

1 East 33rd Street, 4th Floor
New York, NY 10016
Phone: 212-252-8584
Website: www.autismspeaks.org/familyservices
This facet of the Autism Speaks organization offers iPad grants to applicants who need assistive technology.

Babies with iPads

Website: www.babieswithipads.blogspot.com
This blog documents the progress of special needs infants and toddlers as they use an iPad to enhance their development. Through donations, iPads, accessories, and iTunes cards are funded for children with developmental and/or medical issues. The blog also features educational app recommendations.

Conover Company

Website: http://education.conovercompany.com/mobile/grants/
A technology solutions company, Conover offers a Mobile Technology Grant Program to improve an individual's freedom and independence through the use of iPods, iPads, and the company's Functional Skills System apps, which are preloaded on each awarded device. The grants are intended to boost the ability to function independently at home, school, work, and within the community.

Danny's Wish

Website: www.dannyswish.org
Created in honor of a child with autism, Danny's Wish relies on fundraising, sponsorships, and donations to provide life-enhancing experiences for children with autism spectrum disorders.

Gwendolyn Strong Foundation

27 W. Anapamu Street, Suite 177
Santa Barbara, CA 93101
Website: www.thegsf.org/campaigns/detail/projectmariposa
The Gwendolyn Strong Foundation's "Project Mariposa" aims to make the world more accessible to those with severe disabilities through technology product grants for people with spinal muscular atrophy (SMA).

HollyRod Foundation

Website: www.hollyrod.org
This foundation is dedicated to providing a better quality of life for individuals and families living with autism and Parkinson's disease. Through their "Give the Gift of Voice" campaign, tablet computers and specially designed apps are provided so that children with autism who struggle to speak can make their voices heard.

iHelp for Special Needs

5612 Woodview Avenue
Austin, TX 78756
Phone: 254-304-4357
Website: www.ihelpforspecialneeds.com
This organization, formed in honor of a daughter born with Down syndrome, is dedicated to raising funds to provide technology for children with learning delays and special needs. Click on "Need an iPad/App" to learn about their program, or on "Recommended Apps" for apps in categories such as reading and communication.

iTaalk Autism Foundation

2040 W. Central Avenue
Toledo, OH 43606
Phone: 567-377-5710

Website: www.itaalk.org
The iTaalk Autism Foundation works to provide interactive technology education and solutions to individuals with autism and related special needs. The foundation also offers an iPad training series for families and professionals so that children can derive the greatest benefit from their devices.

Little Bear Sees

Website: www.littlebearsees.org/about/charity/little-bear-gives/
Little Bear Sees is devoted to raising awareness about cortical visual impairment (CVI) and providing the information and tools needed to help children with CVI learn how to see. Their Little Bear Gives program aims to provide CVI iPad packages to families who are unable to afford such a device.

The Maggie Welby Foundation

7 Needle Court
Dardenne Prairie, MO 63368
314-330-6947
Website: www.maggiewelby.org/Grants.html
The Maggie Welby Foundation, formed in memory of a beloved seven-year-old, offers grants for a particular purpose to children (grades K–12) and families that have financial need, as well as organizations that benefit children.

Parker's Purpose

1056 Hazel Street
Fremont, OH 43420
Phone: 419-334-7275
Website: www.parkerspurpose.net
Parker's Purpose strives to provide funds and professional services to ill or disabled children who are facing financial need.

Silent Stars

711 Indian Road
Glenview, IL 60025
Phone: 847-644-6591
Website: www.silentstars.org
Silent Stars Foundation was founded to increase awareness of childhood apraxia of speech and raise funds for research and the provision of augmentative communication devices to children in need.

Small Steps in Speech

P.O. Box 65
Eagleville, PA 19408
Phone: 888-577-3256
Website: www.smallstepsinspeech.org
This nonprofit foundation, formed in honor of a deceased serviceman, helps children with speech and language disorders by funding supplemental treatments. It also offers grants to charitable organizations serving children with communication disorders.

Special Kids Therapy

1700 E. Sandusky Drive
Findlay, OH 43585
Phone: 419-422-5607
Website: www.specialkidstherapy.org
This nonprofit charity is dedicated to assisting special needs children and their families in obtaining alternative therapies and quality-of-life necessities through scholarships.

About the Author

Barbara Albers Hill received a BA in Psychology and an MS in Education from Hofstra University in New York. Early in her teaching career, she worked with children and teens with learning disabilities in the Middle Country and New Hyde Park/Garden City Park school districts on Long Island. Later, during a lengthy childrearing hiatus, Ms. Hill began writing articles about young children for *American Baby, Parents, Baby Talk,* and various other parenting magazines. During this time, she also authored and co-authored several books related to infancy, toddlerhood, and childhood.

Ms. Hill returned to the classroom in 1997 and recently concluded her teaching career as a resource specialist in the East Islip school district. She is the co-author of *How to Maximize Your Child's Learning Ability* (Square One, 2004) and *Coping with Concussion and Mild Traumatic Brain Injury* (Penguin Group, 2013), and the co-writer of *The Doctor's Kidney Diet* (Square One, 2014). Ms. Hill and her husband, Kevin, reside on Long Island and are the parents of three adult children.

Index

REVERSING DYSLEXIA
Improving Learning & Behavior Without Drugs
Dr. Phyllis Books

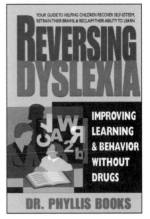

Dyslexia is more than just a reading problem. It is often accompanied by social, emotional, and even physical issues that can make many everyday tasks seem unmanageable. Unfortunately, mainstream treatment focuses on compensatory techniques, often leaving dyslexics feeling hopeless. In this book, Dr. Phyllis Books offers a new approach that can actually reverse dyslexia in a large number of cases.

By providing a modern perspective on dyslexia, this book lays the groundwork for significant improvements not only in reading but also in general learning ability, emotional stability, and psychological well-being. Dr. Books has spent over twenty-five years disproving the idea that dyslexia is a permanent condition. *Reversing Dyslexia* can teach you how to disprove it as well.

$16.95 US • 160 pages • 6 x 9-inch quality paperback • ISBN 978-0-7570-0378-3

THE IRLEN REVOLUTION
A Guide to Changing Your Perception and Your Life
Helen Irlen

After decades of revolutionizing the treatment of dyslexia through the use of colored lenses, Helen Irlen has turned her attention to children and adults who suffer from light sensitivity, headaches, attention deficit disorder, and other visual perception-related conditions and learning disabilities. Here, finally, is hope for everyone who has been misdiagnosed and needs real help for a real problem.

The Irlen Revolution begins by sharing Helen's journey, focusing on her work with struggling readers and detailing how she discovered the Irlen Method. A full description of an Irlen Screening is provided, including home strategies. Finally, the author discusses the individual issues that can get in the way of learning—what they are and how the Irlen Method can treat them. Each chapter deals with a different disability and includes questionnaires that you can use to find the root cause of the difficulty.

$17.95 US • 224 pages • 6 x 9-inch quality paperback • ISBN 978-0-7570-0236-6

THE A.D.D. & A.D.H.D. DIET!

Rachel Bell and Howard Peiper, ND

Every day, children are diagnosed with attention deficit disorder (ADD) or attention deficit hyperactivity disorder (ADHD). Addressing the causes of ADD and ADHD should be the first step in any treatment, but unfortunately, conventional drugs such as Ritalin deal with only the symptoms.

In their new book, *The A.D.D. & A.D.H.D. Diet!,* authors Rachel Bell and Dr. Howard Peiper take a uniquely nutritional approach to treating ADD and ADHD. The authors first address the causes of the disorders, from poor nutrition and food allergies to environmental contaminants. They discuss which foods your child can eat and which foods he should avoid. To make changing your child's diet easier, the authors also offer their very own healthy and delicious recipes. Final chapters examine the importance of detoxifying the body, supplementing diet with vitamins and nutrients, and exercising regularly in order to achieve good health.

$10.95 US • 112 pages • 6 x 9-inch quality paperback • ISBN 978-1-884820-29-8

CREATIVE THERAPY FOR CHILDREN WITH AUTISM, ADD, AND ASPERGER'S

Using Artistic Creativity to Reach, Teach, and Touch Our Children

Janet Tubbs

Thirty years ago, Janet Tubbs began using art, music, and movement to reach children with low self-esteem and behavioral problems. Believing that unconventional children required unconventional therapies, she then applied her program to children with autism, ADD/ADHD, and Asperger's syndrome. Her innovative methods not only worked, but actually defied the experts. In this book, Janet Tubbs has put together a powerful tool to help parents, therapists, and teachers work with their children.

Creative Therapy is divided into two parts. Part One begins by explaining the author's creative approach to balancing a child's body, mind, and spirit through proven techniques. Part Two provides a wide variety of exercises and activities that are both fun and effective. Each is designed to reduce hyperactivity, increase focus, decrease anger, develop fine motor skills, or improve social and verbal skills while helping children relate to their environment without fear or discomfort.

$18.95 US • 336 pages • 7.5 x 9-inch quality paperback • ISBN 978-0-7570-0300-4

THE GENTLE REVOLUTION SERIES

The work performed at The Institutes for the Achievement of Human Potential has demonstrated that children from birth to age six are capable of learning better and faster than older children. Based on these principles, the following books were developed by the Institutes to help children achieve full mental and physical potential and learn basic skills that will serve them for a lifetime. Just as important, these titles were designed to cultivate a young child's awareness of the arts, sciences, and nature. Here is the best-selling parenting series in the United States and the world—with over 13 million copies in print and growing.

HOW TO TEACH YOUR BABY TO READ

Glenn Doman and Janet Doman

$13.95 US • 288 pages • 6 x 9-inch quality paperback

ISBN 978-0-7570-0185-7

HOW TO GIVE YOUR BABY ENCYCLOPEDIC KNOWLEDGE

Glenn Doman, Janet Doman, and Susan Aisen

$13.95 US • 304 pages • 6 x 9-inch quality paperback

ISBN 978-0-7570-0182-6

HOW TO MULTIPLY YOUR BABY'S INTELLIGENCE

Glenn Doman and Janet Doman

$15.95 US • 408 pages • 6 x 9-inch quality paperback

ISBN 978-0-7570-0183-3

HOW TO TEACH YOUR BABY MATH

Glenn Doman and Janet Doman

$13.95 US • 240 pages • 6 x 9-inch quality paperback

ISBN 978-0-7570-0184-0

WHAT TO DO ABOUT YOUR BRAIN-INJURED CHILD

Glenn Doman

In this updated classic, Glenn Doman—founder of The Institutes for the Achievement of Human Potential and pioneer in the treatment of brain-injured children—brings real hope to thousands of children who have been sentenced to a life of institutional confinement.

In *What To Do About Your Brain-Injured Child,* Doman recounts the story of The Institutes' tireless effort to refine treatment of the brain-injured. He shares the staff's lifesaving techniques and the tools used to measure—and ultimately improve—visual, auditory, tactile, mobile, and manual development. Doman explains the unique methods of treatment that are constantly being improved and expanded, and then describes the program with which parents can treat their own children at home in a familiar and loving environment. Included throughout are case histories, drawings, and helpful charts and diagrams.

$18.95 US • 336 pages • 6 x 9-inch quality paperback • ISBN 978-0-7570-0186-4

FIT BABY, SMART BABY, YOUR BABY!

From Birth to Age Six

Glenn Doman, Douglas Doman, and Bruce Hagy

The early development of mobility in newborns is a vital part of their future ability to learn and reach their full potential. We may be wasting our children's most important years by preventing them from physically exploring their world and maximizing their development when they are young—the time when it is easiest for them to grow and learn. In *Fit Baby, Smart Baby, Your Baby!,* Glenn Doman—founder of The Institutes for the Achievement of Human Potential—along with Douglas Doman and Bruce Hagy guide you in expanding the physical capabilities of your child.

Fit Baby, Smart Baby, Your Baby! is an inspiring book that demonstrates how the team of mother, father, and baby can explore and discover together the joys of human mobility. From the simple but vital stage of crawling to the beginnings of the sophisticated skills of the gymnast, this athletic team can make a world of difference to your child.

$18.95 US • 304 pages • 7.5 x 9-inch quality paperback • ISBN 978-0-7570-0376-9

MASSAGING YOUR BABY
The Joy of Touch Time
Elaine Fogel Schneider, PhD

The power of touch is real and has been scientifically shown to have remarkable effects. For infants, it encourages relaxation; improves sleep patterns; reduces discomfort from teething, colic, and gas; strengthens digestive systems; and so much more. For parents, it nurtures bonding, increases communication, promotes parenting skills, and actually reduces stress levels. In *Massaging Your Baby,* massage expert Dr. Elaine Fogel Schneider begins by explaining how and why massage is so beneficial. She then provides an easy-to-follow step-by-step guide to effective massage techniques.

$15.95 US • 224 pages • 7.5 x 9-inch quality paperback • ISBN 978-0-7570-0263-2